UPGRADE Yourself

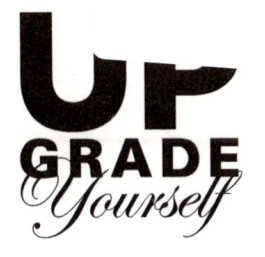

Thibaut Meurisse is a personal development blogger, author and founder of whatispersonaldevelopment.org.

He has been featured on major personal development websites such as Lifehack, Goalcast, TinyBuddha, Addicted2Success, MotivationGrid or PickTheBrain.

Obsessed with self-improvement and fascinated by the power of the brain, his personal mission is to help people realize their full potential and reach higher levels of fulfillment and consciousness.

In love with foreign languages, he is French, writes in English, and lived in Japan for almost a decade.

UPGRADE Yourself

Powerful Strategies to
Transform Your Mindset
and Change Your Life

THIBAUT MEURISSE

Published by
Rupa Publications India Pvt. Ltd 2021
7/16, Ansari Road, Daryaganj
New Delhi 110002

Sales centres:
Allahabad Bengaluru Chennai
Hyderabad Jaipur Kathmandu
Kolkata Mumbai

Copyright © Thibaut Meurisse 2021

The views and opinions expressed in this book are the author's own and
the facts are as reported by him which have been verified to the extent
possible, and the publishers are not in any way liable for the same.

All rights reserved.
No part of this publication may be reproduced, transmitted,
or stored in a retrieval system, in any form or by any means,
electronic, mechanical, photocopying, recording or otherwise,
without the prior permission of the publisher.

ISBN: 978-93-90918-25-6

First impression 2021

10 9 8 7 6 5 4 3 2 1

The moral right of the authors has been asserted.

Printed by HT Media Ltd, Greater Noida

This book is sold subject to the condition that it shall not,
by way of trade or otherwise, be lent, resold, hired out, or otherwise
circulated, without the publisher's prior consent, in any form of binding or
cover other than that in which it is published.

CONTENTS

Introduction	vii
How to Use This Book	ix
Your Free Step-by-Step Workbook	xi
1. Upgrading Your Belief System	1
2. Reprogramming Your Mind	15
3. Changing Your Mindset	21
4. Improving Your Attitude	30
5. Turbocharging Your Vision	37
6. Improving Your Integrity	46
7. Optimizing Your Environment	50
8. Sharpening Your Skills	54
9. Upgrading Your Habits	63
10. Boosting Your Productivity	68
11. Enhancing Self-Discipline	78
12. Taking Care of Your Health	85
13. Mastering Your Emotions	95
14. Cultivating Joy	103
Conclusion	110
Master Your Emotions—Preview	113
Appendix	117

INTRODUCTION

'Here is the big challenge of life: you can have more than you've got, because you can become more than you are. Unless you change how you are, you will always have what you've got.'

—Jim Rohn

We always blame people and circumstances to justify why we aren't where we want to be. It's because of the economy, the government, taxes, our negative relatives or the minimum wage. It's because we don't have enough time or we are too old. Or it's because we aren't smart enough, good enough or talented enough. As personal development expert Jim Rohn once said, 'I found it easier to get rich than I did to make excuses.' What if that's true?

What if the problem is you? What if you aren't giving it 100 per cent? What if you're only giving it 90 per cent, 70 per cent or 30 per cent? What if you need to go the extra mile but haven't committed to it yet?

Unfortunately, most people are operating far below their potential, and that includes you and me. Before we blame external circumstances or people, shouldn't we focus on our personal growth first and see how things change for us? Otherwise, how can we be sure that the problem is external? (It almost never is).

I want this book to remind you of what you already know: you're capable of more! Though your mind is insanely powerful, society has been hijacking it for years; mediocrity has become a disease affecting the majority of people on this planet. We tolerate average as if it's the best we can do. We let the mediocrity of those around us kill our dreams. We allow our friends and family to destroy our potential.

This book is an invitation to step up your game and stop tolerating mediocrity in your life. It's an invitation to go the extra mile and inspire everybody around you; it's a call to honor the power of your mind and live a life without regrets. You can do more, and now is the time to show yourself and the world what you're truly capable of doing.

HOW TO USE THIS BOOK

This book covers 14 different areas. For each area, I'll invite you to go the extra mile and become the best you can be. With this book, I hope to turn you into the best of the best in all (or at least most) of the areas covered.

I encourage you to go through each chapter in order. If you choose to read the book out of order, however, be sure you go over the first chapter before reading any others. It deals with belief systems, so you'll be lost without reading it first.

Each chapter ends with daily mantras. These are affirmations that you can repeat each day to help recondition your mind. Feel free to come up with affirmations of your own. We all react to the same words differently based on our experiences. You'll find explanations on how to create effective affirmations at the end of this book as well as in the corresponding workbook.

Finally, don't hesitate to re-read this book as often as you need to. Repetition is critical when it comes to learning new skills and conditioning your mind.

Are you up to the challenge?

YOUR FREE STEP-BY-STEP WORKBOOK

Before we get started, make sure you download your free workbook available at the following URL:

http://whatispersonaldevelopment.org/upgrade-yourself

If you have any difficulties downloading the workbook, contact me at:

thibaut.meurisse@gmail.com and I will send it to you as soon as possible.

1

UPGRADING YOUR BELIEF SYSTEM

'There are no constraints on the human mind, no walls around the human spirit, no barriers to our progress except those we ourselves erect.'

—Ronald Reagan

Mr Wright had just a few more hours to live. He had tumors throughout this body and couldn't breathe without the help of supplemental oxygen. To say Mr Wright was in bad shape was an understatement. His physician, Dr Klopfer, tried everything he could to save him and was now willing to consider Krebiozen, a new cancer drug, which was still undergoing clinical research. This drug had the potential to be an excellent treatment for cancer. Or so everyone hoped.

Mr Wright begged Dr Klopfer to administer the new drug despite the fact that doing so went against medical protocol. Dr Klopfer complied. A few days later, he was shocked to see Mr Wright walking around the hospital in shockingly good condition. Dr Klopfer ran tests, and the results were almost miraculous. The tumors had shrunk to half their size in just a few days. After only two weeks of using Krebiozen, Mr Wright was tumor-free and soon went home a healthy man.

A couple of months later, the preliminary results of

the clinical trials showed that Krebiozen didn't appear to be effective against cancer. Upon hearing the results of the research, Mr Wright started feeling sick again. His tumors grew back, and he went back into hospitalization.

Dr Klopfer couldn't explain the situation, but he had a sense that it may have had something to do with Mr Wright's beliefs. To test his assumptions, he decided to give Mr Wright injections of sterile water while telling him it was a stronger version of Krebiozen.

Again, Mr Wright's tumors disappeared, and he was able to leave the hospital. However, the American Medical Association eventually reported that Krebiozen didn't work. One headline even declared, 'Nationwide Tests Show Krebiozen to Be a Worthless Drug in the Treatment of Cancer.' Mr Wright was shocked, and his tumors reappeared. He died shortly after.

Mr Wright's situation may be an extreme case, but if a person's thoughts have the power to make tumors disappear, imagine what you could do with your own beliefs!

Changing Your Belief System

You can't go the extra mile and transform your life without changing your belief system. Think of your belief system as a program that runs in the background without your knowledge. It determines what's possible for you. In fact, we all live our lives according to our unique belief systems, for better or worse. As the spiritual teacher, Mooji, says, 'There is one earth, but billions of worlds.'

Your programming (belief system) leads you to have specific thoughts; these thoughts generate emotions, and these feelings compel you to take particular actions. Eventually, what you do determines the results you get in life.

Most people have fully formed belief systems once they reach adulthood, and they usually keep the same ones for the rest of their lives. They never change their beliefs regarding the world. Their political opinions remain the same, their vision of themselves stays static, and their religious beliefs never change. They seldom question what they believe, and instead behave as if their views are entirely correct. This assumption couldn't be further from the truth.

One thing that I find fascinating about human beings is that each of us believes we're right. Gandhi thought he was right, and so did Hitler. You think you're right, too, don't you?

I have bad news for you. No belief is fundamentally right. None of us hold the 'correct' opinions. In fact, viewpoints are merely a human thing. The universe couldn't care less about your beliefs. It exists independently of them and doesn't give a damn what you choose to believe.

I'm not going to get into a complicated metaphysical theory here. What I want to show you is that beliefs aren't set in stone and are ultimately neither true nor false. As such, you're free to change what you believe and adopt a new, empowering belief system at any given time. Isn't that exciting?

Your beliefs don't need to be correct; they just need to support you in designing the life you want. It's as simple as that. With that in mind, the fundamental questions you want to ask yourself are, 'Do my current beliefs serve me? Are they helping me live a better life?' If not, why are you hanging onto them?

The Origins of Your Belief System

Your current belief system was created based on past information you received from parents, teachers or the media. You accepted them as true on a subconscious level because you weren't in a position to choose to reject them. Your belief system is also the result of beliefs you formed due to emotionally charged experiences, such as a childhood trauma.

Fortunately, you now have the power to choose what to believe and can eliminate any belief that has become irrelevant. The limiting ideas that have been holding you back could be about money, relationships, spirituality or even yourself. Life is about getting rid of limiting beliefs and adopting new, empowering ones that will help you move forward. See your belief system as a costume you wear. If you don't like it, change it.

Still not convinced of how powerful what you believe is? Let me give you a concrete example of how our environment and upbringing shapes our beliefs.

Let's say you were born into an extremely religious family and had become very religious yourself. Let's also assume that your family taught you that your religion was the only correct one. You would probably believe that, wouldn't you?

Now, imagine a scenario, in which an extremely religious family who practised a different religion adopted you at birth. In this situation, your family also teaches you that your faith is the only correct one. What do you think your religious beliefs would be? Wouldn't you believe that this other religion was the only one that's right? I bet you would. Whose opinion is correct, then? No one's!

That's how powerful a belief can be. It can convince you

that you're right no matter what you choose to believe and regardless of the external reality. In the end, a belief is merely a subjective interpretation of the outside world. It's neither right nor wrong.

What's Your Personal Story?

What is your current belief system? How does it impact the decisions you make? Is it limiting you or is it empowering you?

We're all telling ourselves a particular story. Your story can empower you or destroy your ability to create the life you want. As Mooji said, 'A thought without belief has no power, a thought with belief can start a war.'

Your personal story works similarly. Buy into the wrong narrative, and it can make your life miserable. Change it, and you'll suddenly feel empowered. A few years from now you could even find yourself achieving things that you didn't even think were possible.

So what's your story? Is it the story of a hero or heroine who's moving towards their goals with confidence and excitement? Or is it the story of a victim who feels powerless?

In the grand scheme of things, both stories are false. The universe doesn't care which one you choose to believe, but I would guess that you care.

If you want to transform your life, you need to take an honest look at your personal story and make a firm commitment to rewrite it in a way that better suits your vision. You are what you believe, so don't buy into anyone else's beliefs. Choose your own, and do so carefully!

Remember: your beliefs are a scenario you can rewrite, a costume you can change, an identity you can alter.

So what about you? How strong are your beliefs?

When it comes to success, your beliefs are one of the most critical factors. They are what will drive your actions and determine your level of perseverance. They can be the difference between an average person and an exceptional one.

Think of the most significant dream you have. Do you genuinely believe you can achieve it, or do you hope that one day, if you're lucky, you might attain it? Would you be willing to bet $100 that you'll make your dream come true? What about $1,000 or $10,000? What does your answer say about your level of certainty?

What's Holding You Back?

Why haven't you achieved the results you want in life? What's holding you back?

You must have written your story in a way that prevents you from living the life you want. There must be a set of specific beliefs that are working against you. What are they?

Below are some examples of common limiting beliefs you may currently hold:

- I don't know the right people.
- I don't have enough time.
- I don't have enough money.
- I'm not smart enough.
- I'm too shy.
- I'm not confident enough.
- I don't have any talent.
- I won't be happy until such and such happens.
- There's too much competition.
- I'm too old.

- I'm too young.
- I don't know how to do it.

And the list goes on and on.

How to Identify Your Limiting Beliefs

To discover your limiting beliefs, look at each area of your life and ask yourself why you aren't where you want to be. Then list your reasons. Check out the example below:

1. Why aren't I where I want to be regarding finances?
    - I'm not smart enough.
    - I don't have enough time to work on my side business.
    - Money is the root of all evil.
2. Why haven't I attracted the man or woman of my dreams?
    - I'm not attractive.
    - I'm disinteresting.
    - I need money to attract a partner.
    - I don't have the time to go out.
    - I don't like parties.
3. Why don't I have the career I want?
    - I don't have the right education.
    - I don't know the right people.
    - I don't know what I need to do.
    - I don't have enough time.
    - My friends and family aren't supportive.

Do you hold any of the limiting beliefs mentioned above?

Using Your Emotions to Identify Your Beliefs

You can pinpoint your limiting beliefs by investigating specific feelings that you experience on a consistent basis. Do you feel angry on a regular basis? Do you feel sad? Do you feel frustrated? If so, ask yourself this: what would I need to believe to feel that emotion?

The negative emotions you experience are the result of your beliefs. You feel a certain way because you have certain assumptions or expectations regarding how things should be. When things aren't the way you want them to be, you suffer.

Let me give you a personal example. I'm sometimes frustrated when people who promise to help me let me down. Now, what would I need to believe to feel that frustration? Below are some of the beliefs I may have:

- People should keep their promises.
- People are disrespecting me when they don't keep their promises.
- They know how important this is to me.

Now, let's have a look at a specific process you can use to overcome your limiting beliefs.

A 7-Step Process to Overcome Limiting Beliefs

1. Challenging your limiting beliefs

When you believe something, it's because you stopped questioning it and became convinced that it's true. As such, challenging your beliefs is the first step to overcoming them.

Start by picking one of your most prominent limiting beliefs. Now, imagine that your limiting belief is a table, and its four legs are some of your current assumptions.

Let's come back to the previous example about people who reneged on their promises. This belief would represent the table. The four legs (assumptions) could be:

1. People should do what they promise.
2. When someone says they'll help me, it means they're fully committed to doing so.
3. What I'm asking for is as important to them as it is to me.
4. People are 100 per cent reliable and should never make mistakes.

Are these assumptions true? Is it possible that I misinterpreted things? Let's look at the assumptions one at a time to see whether they're correct. One way to do that is to consider the viewpoint of those who promised to help and try to think from their perspective.

- What if it wasn't a real commitment to them?
- What if they thought that what I asked them wasn't important at all? Sure, it's important to me, but they're probably busy and have other priorities.
- What if they just forgot about it? After all, nobody is perfect.

2. Turning things around

Another strategy is to direct the questions to myself and see what I would do in a similar situation:

1. I should keep my promises - Yes. I believe I should, but it doesn't mean I'm 100 per cent reliable. I wish it did, but that's not the case.
2. In the past, whenever I said I would help someone, I was committed to it. - Do I sometimes say yes to something without following through on it? Certainly.

There are situations in which people may believe I'm committed, but from my point of view, I'm not.
3. I consider what they ask me to be as important as they do. - Probably not. When someone asks me for a favor, it's very likely that it's more important to them than it is to me. After all, it's something they need, not something I need.
4. I'm 100 per cent reliable and never make mistakes. - Of course not. As much as I would like this to be true, it isn't. I'm human, and sometimes I forget to do something or I get lazy.

3. Looking for counter-examples

The next step is to look at specific examples where I didn't do what I said I would do. I can think of a lot of cases where I didn't deliver something on time or didn't follow through on a commitment.

4. Looking at the consequences of your belief

What are the effects of holding your limiting belief? How does it make you feel? How much suffering does it create in your life? Often, it's when you're sick and tired that you finally commit to making the necessary changes in your life. Eliciting strong negative emotions will help you create new empowering beliefs and get rid of the old ones.

The angrier you get about having bought into that stupid belief your whole life, the better you'll be able to overcome it and replace it with a new, empowering one. Doesn't it piss you off to have a belief that has been holding you back for so many years? It should!

Take a moment to think of how your belief has been

holding you back. Now, do you want to continue living your life this way? Do you want to allow this thought to control all areas of your life? Or do want you want to take control of what you believe and start changing your life?

5. Envisioning who you would be without that belief

Now, imagine if you could use a magic wand to remove that belief entirely. How would that make you feel? What kind of person would you be without that belief?

Remember that a belief is like a costume you wear. It's an identity you give to yourself. If you don't like what you're wearing, you can change it. That's one of the incredible powers of the human mind. You can plant new seeds (thoughts) in it at any time. These new seeds will give birth to a new tree (belief) that will bear fruit (results obtained by the actions you took based on what you now believe).

6. Coming up with a new, empowering belief

Limiting beliefs are like bad habits; they don't disappear on their own. They have to be replaced by something better. Once you identify a limiting belief, you want to substitute it for a new, empowering one. Look at your limiting belief and ask yourself, what would be the opposite of that?

For instance:

- I don't have the time to start a business → I find and make time for whatever I'm committed to.
- I'm not smart enough → I'm as capable as anyone else and I can always learn more, grow, and improve.
- I'm not confident → I can sometimes lack confidence, but I can also be very self-confident depending on the situation.

7. Validating your new empowering belief

The next step is to strengthen your new belief. One way to do that is by looking at examples that prove it.

It could be:

- Role models or people who show that your new, empowering belief is justified.
- Past examples in your personal life that show your new belief is correct.

Let's say your new belief is 'I find and make time for whatever I'm committed to.' You might look online for people who successfully created a business despite a hectic schedule and lots of personal responsibilities.

You might also want to look at people to whom you can easily relate. If you're a single mom who wants to start an online business, for instance, look for other single moms who created successful businesses. If you search hard enough, I'm pretty sure you'll find single moms with multiple children who managed to build successful companies. So why not you?

The more you look at examples that validate your new, empowering belief, the more you'll realize that most of your limiting beliefs are false. Do you think you're too old to run a marathon? Well, the oldest person to finish a marathon was over 100. Do you think you're too shy or lack confidence and that you'll never be able to overcome it? You'll find people who were extremely shy and become insanely confident. If they can do it, why can't you?

I like to believe that other people are no smarter than me. If they can do it, I can do it, too. I highly encourage you to adopt a similar belief.

Another way to validate your new, empowering belief is to

look at past examples from your own life. If you believe that you don't have time to start a business, can you think of a time in the past when you were overwhelmingly busy but managed to achieve your goals due to your commitment to them? These could be relationship goals, financial goals, health goals, etc. If so, can't you find and make the time for a new commitment?

Do you believe you lack confidence? Well, aren't there areas in your life in which you feel confident? Maybe you feel confident when you play sports. Or perhaps it's when you cook. You don't lack confidence. You already have confidence; you just need to spread it out to more areas in your life. Or maybe there was a time in the past when you felt confident. What were you doing? Why were you feeling that way?

Final tip: Remember that your mind likes to generalize things. That's why we hold so many stereotypes. To be able to understand the world, our brain needs to label things and classify them. The same goes for your beliefs. Your beliefs are generalizations that do not accurately reflect reality. They don't need to, but you want them to serve you, not to work against you.

Watch out for words like 'always' or 'never.' These are signs that you're making generalizations. Nothing is ever black and white, and the first step towards changing your beliefs is realizing that they aren't as reliable as you think they are. They aren't cast in concrete, and you can change them at any time. Take some time to analyse them, and before long you'll realize how baseless they are. Look at the following beliefs:

- I never have time.
- I've never had confidence.
- I'm not good at anything.

Now, what happens if you replace 'I never have time' with 'I do have some time, but I'm not always using it the right way' or 'I do have time, and it's my responsibility to use it effectively?' Or 'I'll make the time for whatever matters to me!'

What if you replace 'I've never had confidence' with 'There are situations in which I lack confidence, but there are also situations in which I feel confident?'

As for the third belief, is it true that you aren't good at anything? Not one, single thing? I doubt it. You could replace that statement with 'There are things I'm not good at, but there are also things I do well.' Don't forget that you can always grow and learn. We all have thousands of things we suck at, and that's perfectly normal. There's nothing to be ashamed of here.

The bottom-line is this: you don't need to get overly attached to your limiting beliefs. They aren't nearly as real as you think they are. As I said before, beliefs are like costumes. If you don't like what you're currently wearing, change into something else.

Here's another fabulous belief to adopt:

I can overcome any limiting beliefs no matter what they are.

Action Step:

Spend a few minutes completing the corresponding exercise in the workbook (I. Updating your Belief system)

2

REPROGRAMMING YOUR MIND

'A human being always acts and feels and performs in accordance with what he imagines to be true about himself and his environment... For imagination sets the goal "picture" which our automatic mechanism works on. We act, or fail to act, not because of "will", as is so commonly believed, but because of imagination.'

—Maxwell Maltz

An excellent way to overcome limiting beliefs and experience more joy in your life is to condition your mind daily. Sadly, your brain is not designed to make you happy. Your brain is designed to ensure your survival, and that's the reason you're here today. Your mind makes sure that you feel good after you eat, drink, have sex or do something that feels safe, preserves your life or increases our population. That way, you won't die from hunger, thirst or putting yourself in danger, and you'll be likely to pass on your genes. Aside from that, however, your brain won't help with your happiness unless you train it to do so.

The wiring of your brain is mostly obsolete. We no longer have to risk our lives for food each day and dangerous animals aren't lurking behind every corner anymore. Even so, our brains continuously scan the environment for potential threats.

As such, your brain is wired to focus on the negative. Have you noticed how just one negative comment about your work can outweigh the hundreds of positive comments you've received? That's probably because of the way your brain functions. It perceives anything that can lead to being ostracized or rejected as a threat.

As silly as this may seem today, avoiding rejection was very important for the bulk of human history. In the past, being expelled from one's community could mean exposure to the elements, a decrease in the ability to hunt and ultimately, death. Nowadays, things are entirely different. Expulsion from one's community is rare, and it wouldn't be a death sentence if it were to happen.

Even so, our brains are still looking for potential threats and the possibility of rejection. It's as if the brain has learned to redirect its focus from significant risks to minor ones. It often perceives anything that carries even the remote possibility of rejection as a threat.

You can test this out for yourself. Look at your negative emotions and fears. You'll notice that many of them involve fear of rejection and the desire to belong. Your boss criticizes your work? Fear instantly kicks in. On a subconscious level, you begin to think the worst. What if you get fired and can't find another job? If that happens, your spouse and kids will likely leave you and you'll eventually become homeless. Sooner than later, you'll die on the streets and no one will remember your existence. Pretty scary, isn't it?

As Mark Twain said, 'most of what we worry about will never happen.' The media, politicians and marketers love to play on our fears because it makes us more vulnerable and easier to manipulate. Fear sells, not rational arguments. Did you know that people buy more products after seeing negative news than they otherwise would have? It's crazy but true! No wonder we're inundated with bad news and all things fear-inducing.

Creating a Morning Ritual to Condition Your Mind

Fortunately, we have the power to condition our minds to experience more positive emotions. We can stop being enslaved by our fears. After all, most of us are living in relatively safe environments and have a myriad of things for which we can be grateful. Why should we waste our time and energy on a negative mindset?

The best way I've found to condition my mind is through my daily morning ritual. Many successful people have a daily morning ritual. For some, it might be spending time meditating, for others it might be writing down their goals or expressing gratitude for what they have.

The popularity of morning rituals has recently increased thanks to Hal Elrod's best-selling book *Miracle Morning*. My book *Wake Up Call* is devoted entirely to morning rituals. In it, I share my personal experiences and help my readers implement an invigorating morning ritual in 10 simple steps.

Stefan Pylarinos also has a fantastic video course called 'Morning Ritual Mastery.' I've used his program to create my morning ritual, and I highly recommend it. You can learn more about it here.

You'll also find plenty of fantastic videos online for free. For instance, you can check the quick video I made on how to create a morning ritual here.

The Benefits of a Morning Ritual

A daily morning ritual will do the following:

- **Help you condition your mind.** Implementing a morning ritual will help you condition your mind to experience more of the emotions that you wish to focus on. For instance, I want to experience more gratitude and peace of mind in my life, so I spend time meditating and expressing gratitude each day. It helps me wake up happy rather than starting my day feeling depressed or demotivated.
- **Ensure you stick to your daily habits.** A daily morning ritual is a terrific way to stack all your excellent habits together. Imagine how your life would improve if you combined several great daily habits. Personally, I stack my meditation practice, gratitude exercise and goal-setting habits together.
- **Help you build momentum.** It ensures that you don't lose momentum by skipping your habits.
- **Help you overcome your limiting beliefs.** You can use your morning ritual to overcome your limiting beliefs. You can repeat affirmations for 5 to 10 minutes. These affirmations are similar to the new, empowering beliefs we discussed in the previous section. An example would be 'I find and make the time for whatever I'm committed to.' Make sure that you engage your emotions and use visualization to increase the effectiveness of your affirmations.[*]

A Crash Course in Creating a Morning Ritual

You can create your customized morning ritual to help you condition your mind and get rid of limiting beliefs. Read on

---

*See free worksheet on affirmations at the end of the workbook.

for the nine steps from my book *Wake Up Call*. These nine items will help you create a morning ritual that will support you in achieving your goals.

1. **Clarifying your 'why'**: Make sure you have a clear objective in mind when you create your morning ritual. It might be particular emotions that you want to experience or a specific goal that you'd like to focus on with affirmations or visualization.
2. **Getting excited about your morning ritual**: Make sure your morning ritual is something that genuinely excites you. Drink your favorite coffee, read your favorite book or spend time with your family. Do whatever works for you.
3. **Identifying obstacles and preparing yourself mentally**: Identify potential hurdles you may encounter as you create your morning ritual. If you tried and failed to implement a morning ritual in the past, ask yourself why.
4. **Selecting the components of your morning ritual**: For a more balanced morning ritual, select activities that will feed your body, mind and soul. Try exercise, meditation, journaling and things of that nature.
5. **Deciding how much time you have available**: Decide how much time you want to dedicate to your morning ritual each day. It could 10 minutes, 30 minutes or even an hour.
6. **Removing roadblocks and distractions**: Make sure you remove all distractions. Prepare everything you need the night before. Go through your morning ritual first thing in the morning to avoid procrastination.
7. **Setting yourself up for success**: Make sure you get enough sleep. If necessary, create an evening ritual as

well. Whenever possible, go to bed at the same time every night. You can also set your intentions the night before and visualize the tasks you want to work on the next day.
8. **Committing 100 per cent**: Commit to your morning ritual. Don't be casual about it.
9. **Undertaking the 30-Day Challenge**: To strengthen your commitment, dedicate 30 days to your morning ritual.

Are you ready to implement a morning ritual that will inspire you to make changes in your life?

If you want to learn more about how to create an exciting morning ritual, check out my book *Wake Up Call: How to Take Control of Your Morning and Transform Your life.*

Your Daily Mantras

Repeat the following mantra on a daily basis:
I can overcome any limiting beliefs no matter what they are.

Action Step:

Spend a few minutes completing the corresponding exercise in the workbook (II. Reprogramming your Mind)

3

CHANGING YOUR MINDSET

'Everything you people have told me. I didn't have the technology, I didn't have the right contacts, I didn't have the time, I didn't have the money. Everything you told me, those are resources. And so you're telling me: "I failed because I didn't have the resources" and I'm here to tell you what you already know: resources are never the problem, it's a lack of resourcefulness. This is why you failed. Because the ultimate resources are emotional states: creativity, decisiveness, passion, honesty, sincerity, love. These are the ultimate human resources, and when you engage these resources you can get any other resources on earth.'

—Tony Robbins

Picture this: you just woke up from a long coma and can't remember anything. You don't even know your name. You're trying hard to figure out who the people in your hospital room are. All you're aware of is the fact that you've been in the hospital for five years. A man tells you how much your team has missed you. 'What team?' you ask, only to be informed that you're a respected Navy SEAL officer. The man smiles and tells you that your team can't wait for you to return.

After months and months of rehabilitation and training, you're finally ready to go back to your previous position as a SEAL officer. The training was so demanding that there were many times when you thought of giving up, but you didn't; you couldn't help but remember that you went through similar training in the past. If you've done it before, you can do it again, right? And you can't let down your team, can you?

There's just one problem, though. You were never a Navy SEAL. In reality, you worked at a bank.

This fictional story shows you how your beliefs about yourself impact your life. If you had no memory of your life and believed that you used to be a Navy SEAL, wouldn't you behave differently than you would if you thought you had been a schoolteacher? How much more perseverant would you be? How much more grit do you think you'd have? How much more confident would you be?

Creating an Exceptional Mindset

To reach a higher level of success, you must go beyond changing your belief system. You must also transform your mindset by acquiring new mental habits that will support your goals. These mental habits include perseverance, confidence, determination, proactivity, commitment and consistency.

Many people fail to achieve their goals not because they lack talent, aren't smart enough or don't know the right people, but because they have the wrong mindset. Most of the excuses we use in our daily lives make us feel good about ourselves. They keep us from looking in the mirror and realizing that the reason we aren't where we want to be is our less than optimal mindset. In other words, we lack resourcefulness. Not resources, but resourcefulness. That's why we fall short of our goals.

Imagine what you could do if you had an insane ability to persevere through any challenge or obstacle you encounter. Imagine if procrastination were a non-issue and you could motivate yourself to accomplish any task even when you don't feel like doing it. These are examples of mental habits, all of which you can develop over time.

My levels of perseverance, self-discipline and confidence have skyrocketed since starting my online business three years ago. It didn't happen overnight, though. In fact, I almost gave up on it less than a year after I started it. No. It was a conscious choice I made. I realized that achieving my goals would come at a price. I realized I would have to become more consistent, more disciplined, more perseverant, and more patient. I then started developing these skills.

We'll talk more about self-discipline when we enter the corresponding section in this book. For now, let's focus on a key concept, the mastery mindset.

Developing a Mastery Mindset

'One reason so few of us achieve what we truly want is that we never direct our focus; we never concentrate our power. Most people dabble their way through life, never deciding to master anything in particular.'

—Tony Robbins

Developing a mastery mindset will allow you to get significantly better results in all areas of your life.

Most people fail to achieve the results they want because

they hold incorrect assumptions about what it takes to succeed. Before you work on developing a mastery mindset, it's essential to look deeper into some of your beliefs.

Components of the Mastery Mindset

Now that you have a better sense of what a mastery mindset entails let's have a look at its main components.

1. Focusing on the process

It's important to focus on the process of success each day. Doing so is crucial to getting the results you want. That means repeating specific tasks on a regular basis to achieve your goal. Repetition is the mother of skill mastery. Without it, you'll remain a dabbler who will never truly master anything. A dabbler mentality will prevent you from raising your standards and becoming your best.

Someone with a mastery mindset trusts the process and puts a system in place that ensures they will achieve their goal. They have a great deal of patience because they understand that anything worthwhile takes time.

2. Thinking long-term

Adopting a mastery mindset means that you must get rid of short-term thinking and stop looking for get-rich-quick schemes. No, you won't become a millionaire in 30 days by buying a $49 program online. If that were the case, do you think they would be selling the product for just $49? Again, people severely underestimate the power of patience, and lack of it is one of the main reasons people fail to achieve their goals.

3. Being extremely focused

Do you jump from one course to another, one seminar to the next or one diet to another? Focusing on too many things at once is one of the biggest mistakes people make. Unfortunately, you can't master several things at the same time. If you try to chase two rabbits at once, you'll end up catching none. Once you identify something you wish to focus on for next few years, stick to it. Don't give up after 6 to 12 months because you didn't get the results you wanted.

Let me tell you a dirty secret: when you start something new, you'll have unrealistic expectations and will fail to achieve your original target. Sometimes you'll be far off. That's part of the process, so don't get too upset by it. Instead, persevere and remain focused on your target.

4. Applying everything you learn

How often have you bought a program without following through with it? At the 2015 IDPF/BE conference, Kobo disclosed data that shows 60 per cent of books purchased are never even opened! According to research conducted by an Open University doctoral student, the average completion rate for open online courses is less than 7 per cent. That means 93 per cent of students who enrolled in such programs never completed them.

While many programs out there don't deliver what they promise, there are also countless great programs that will help you get the results you want. Adopting a mastery mindset and applying everything you learn instead of dabbling is what will determine your level of success.

5. Going back to basics

How often do you catch yourself saying 'But I already know that'? Most people believe they know things just because they have an intellectual understanding of them. That's why most people get stuck and fail to get the results they want. They think they know things when they don't. You can't learn to drive a car by reading a book about it. You can't become a great manager by merely going through case studies. You won't become a great conversationalist just by spending hours every day reading a book on the subject.

Similarly, you won't achieve excellent results in your life by reading a book that tells you to raise your standards and go the extra mile. Knowledge without action is just mental masturbation.

We like to make things complicated, but the truth is that taking action will solve many problems. Nike is right with its famous, 'Just do it' slogan. You'll be better off spending all of your time taking action without reading a book than you will be reading books without taking action. Of course, I still recommend reading some books, too!

Master vs. Dabbler

Once someone with the mastery mindset buys a program, they know that they'll get results most of the time. The 'master' will tend to do the following:

- Commit 100 per cent until they get results
- Pay full price for the program if needed (they aren't obsessed with getting things cheaply or for free)
- Apply everything they learn before moving on to the next lesson

- Be consistent
- Go over previous topics again and again if they fail to get results
- Stick to one or two programs maximum

The average person will do the following:

- Never really commit to anything
- Pay as little as possible for the program
- Go through lessons one after the other feeling pumped up even if they aren't absorbing the information
- Skip all or part of the exercises mentioned in the program (by the way, this person probably won't make it until the end of the program)
- Blame the program or the creator of the program when they don't get results (they might even ask for a refund)
- Go through several programs at once

If you want to have one of the strongest mindsets of your peers, it's essential that you 'master' the Mastery Mindset.

The Bullet-Proof Timeframe

Creating an exceptional mindset requires the development of a vital skill: patience. Yes, I like to think of patience as a skill, as I believe you can develop it over time. Since it's a skill, there's no need to worry if it's an area where you struggle. In fact, lack of patience is a weakness of mine. That's why I regularly have to refocus on the process and trust it. Fortunately, I've made significant progress in the past couple of years.

Patience makes the difference between someone who consistently works on their goal for five years and someone who is inconsistent and gives up within a couple of months or years. Remember that mastery takes time. The real growth comes when you stick to your goals for more than two years.

I've found it useful to set a specific timeframe, which I call the 'Bullet-Proof Timeframe'. I commit to working on my primary goal during this period. A two or three-year timeline is ideal.

For instance, I've committed myself to writing books consistently until 18 April 2020, which is my 35th birthday. While many things may go wrong and unexpected things will happen (like losing all the data on my computer including drafts of two books. True story!), I will not break that commitment because I understand that mastery takes time.

Implementing a Bullet-Proof Timeframe will do more than help you stay patient. It will also ensure that you set a genuinely significant goal. Would you commit 100 per cent to a goal for the next two to three years if you weren't all that excited about it? Probably not.

A Bullet-Proof Timeframe will help you overcome your tendency to give up. Indeed, when you set a Bullet-Proof Timeframe, you also give yourself total permission to give up once you reach it. Yes, you can give up all you want once you hit the end date, but NEVER before. That's the trick.

Of course, just because you didn't get the results you expected doesn't mean that you should give up on your goal once you've reached the end of your Bullet-Proof Timeframe. But at least the option will be on the table. Until then, the only thing you have to do is stay focused on your goal.

The Benefits of the Bullet-Proof Timeframe

Below are the main benefits you'll get from adopting a Bullet-Proof Timeframe. Your Bullet-Proof Timeframe will do the following:

- **Boost your patience.** By setting a clear 'deadline' and giving yourself a specific window during which you will focus on your goal, you send a clear signal to your mind that you have time.
- **Entice you to set a goal that genuinely excites you.** You can't commit to an unexciting goal for an extended period. The Bullet-Proof Timeframe gives you an opportunity to reflect on your goals and one that's truly meaningful.
- **Reduce self-sabotage and increase your ability to persevere.** As you permit yourself to give up after you reach the deadline, you can more easily overcome your tendency to give up too soon. After all, you can always give up later. Effectively, you are delaying giving up so that you can focus on your goal.

Your Daily Mantras:

Repeat the following mantras on a daily basis:

- My mindset is exceptional. I master everything I decide to learn.
- I'm always learning, growing, and improving.
- My mind is the most resilient tool in the world.

Action Step:

Spend a few minutes completing the corresponding exercise in the workbook (III. Changing your Mindset)

4

IMPROVING YOUR ATTITUDE

'Your attitude, not your aptitude, will determine your altitude.'

—Zig Ziglar

Along with your beliefs, your attitude is one of the most important things you can cultivate in your life. Your beliefs and attitude will largely determine the results you get in life. So it goes without saying that going the extra mile means adopting a great attitude.

What is Attitude?

Read the two following quotes (You'll see why later)

'I love living life. I'm happy.'

—Nick Vujicic

'I was always laughing. We were lying on the floor with my son, and he saw me laughing. How can a child not laugh when the mother laughs?'

—Alice Herz Sommer

Your attitude is just how you choose to act and react in your day-to-day life. Highly successful people are proactive. Average people are reactive. Highly successful people take 100 per cent responsibility for their actions. Average people blame their circumstances.

If you want to step up your game and take it to the next level, you must upgrade your attitude and take absolute responsibility for everything that happens in your life.

Your attitude is essential because it's all you have! We all face challenges in life, but in the end, they don't determine the most critical parts of your life. Many people could have chosen to give up in the face of adversity, but they didn't. The question isn't whether we'll fall. The question is whether we'll get back up. As Jim Rohn said, 'It's not what happens that determines the major part of your future. What happens, happens to us all. It is what you do about what happens that counts.' That's what attitude is in a nutshell. Attitude is how you choose to react to what happens to you.

Choosing Your Attitude

Do you choose your attitude or do you react to everything that happens to you? Most people go through life responding to people and circumstances. They fail to realize that they have absolute control over their attitude. There are many things in our environment that we cannot control, but we can always choose how we react to what happens to us.

Let me give you some examples. If I were to insult you, how would you react? Would you insult me back? Would you hate me? Most people would consider those normal reactions, but I don't. For me, responding to people who have a poor attitude means stooping to their level. I don't have to do that. I have a choice. I can choose how to act and react at any moment. The last thing I want is for someone else to infect me with their poor attitude.

I want to avoid the typical and highly mechanical reactions that we see every day. For example:

- You hate me; I hate you
- You insult me; I insult you
- You disrespect me; I disrespect you
- You greet me; I greet you, you don't greet me; I don't greet you

Where is the free will here?

Here's a great question to ask yourself: would I do the same thing in a typical situation? For instance, if that person didn't insult you, would you insult them out of the blue? If they weren't impolite, would you be rude to them? The answer is probably no. Why would you let someone negatively impact *your* attitude?

I encourage you to see your attitude as something that you choose and then stick to it. You have your standards, and nobody around you can negatively impact your attitude without your permission.

Choosing your attitude is extremely important because it allows you to maintain your power instead of giving it away to people and circumstances. What happens, happens, and the behavior of others is their problem, not yours. Choosing your attitude is not about the other person. It's about self-respect, understanding that you owe yourself a great attitude and knowing you're in charge of your destiny.

Taking 100 per cent Responsibility for Your Life

Choosing your attitude also means taking 100 per cent responsibility for your life. You refuse to give even an ounce of your power away. I've never seen a highly successful person who didn't take responsibility for their actions. You are responsible for each area of your life. If you aren't happy with your current results, it's your responsibility to make the necessary changes. If you can do something about it, it's your job to accept reality rather than blame external factors for your problems.

Do you remember the two quotes at the beginning of this chapter?

'I love living life. I'm happy.'

—Nick Vujicic

'I was always laughing. We were lying on the floor with my son, and he saw me laughing. How can a child not laugh when the mother laughs?'

—Alice Herz Sommer

What if I told you that Nick Vujicic was born without arms and legs and that Alice Herz Sommer was describing her experience in a concentration camp?

Nick Vujicic could have been bitter and blamed the world. No one would have blamed him for that. In truth, he spent his youth thinking he would never be happy. However, at some point, he had to accept reality and take responsibility for his life. That worked out well for him, as he's now a happily married father of one.

Alice Herz Sommer could have been miserable. Nobody

would have blamed her, either. After all, she spent time starving in a concentration camp never knowing if she would survive the day. Like Nick Vujicic, she accepted reality and chose to see the good in life rather than focus on the negative. In their situation, it must have been beyond challenging, and it's unlikely that you'll ever have to face similar scenarios. However, they are both living proof that you always have a choice. Always. Even in the worst of situations.

How Responsibility Empowers You

> *'You are where you are because of who you are. If you want to be somewhere else, you're gonna have to change something.'*
>
> —Eric Thomas

- How can you change something that you refuse to take responsibility for?
- You can't improve your relationship if you believe everything is your partner's fault.
- You can't change your finances if you believe they're the result of the economy, the political system or something of that nature.
- You can't overcome shyness if you believe it's who you are and refuse to admit that it's up to you to change it.

See what I mean?

Taking full responsibility for your life requires being brutally honest with yourself. You need to look at each area of your life and ask yourself the following question: how am I responsible for my current situation?

As a rule of thumb, the more you take responsibility in your life, the more power you have to change it.

Taking Extra Responsibility

Looking for ways in which you may be responsible for your situation is a powerful tool for growth. We're often responsible for more than we'd like to admit. Perhaps you ask someone to do some work for you, but they fail to deliver what you expect of them. Your first reaction might be to see that person as incompetent. Now, ask yourself, *what is my part in this?* Maybe you didn't communicate what you wanted well enough. Or perhaps you didn't do your research and asked the wrong person to do the job. If you think about things like this, you'll start to realize that you could have done things differently and that the situation isn't all the other person's fault.

There will be some situations in which you may have no responsibility whatsoever. But even then you need to ask yourself what part you might have played in it. Doing this will help you discover insights about yourself and increase your self-awareness. It's also a great way to train yourself to anticipate problems before they arise and, as a result, make better decisions.

You should always strive to take more responsibility in your life. It's the only way to take your power back. When it comes to personal responsibility, go the extra mile and always ask yourself what part you've played in any given situation.

Remember that the idea here isn't to beat yourself up. The point is to realize that you may be partially responsible for many of the events that occur in your life. It's incredibly empowering and will allow you to make positive changes in your life.

Your Daily Mantras:

Repeat the following mantras on a daily basis:

- I'm in total control of my attitude at all times.
- I enjoy taking full responsibility for my life. I'm the creator of my existence.
- I love choosing the way I react to everything that happens to me.

Action Step:

Spend a few minutes completing the corresponding exercise in the workbook (IV. Improving your Attitude)

5

TURBOCHARGING YOUR VISION

'The only thing worse than being blind is having sight but no vision.'

—Hellen Keller

Imagine walking by a construction site with three workers. Let's say you ask the first man what he's doing, and he replies that he's laying bricks. You ask the second worker, who says that he's building a wall. The third and final man seems surprisingly happy when you ask him what he's doing, and replies that he's making an incredible, majestic house.

Here's a question for you: are you laying bricks or are you building an incredible, majestic house? In other words, do you wake up inspired every day? Do you feel like you're making a difference? Or do you wake up depressed and wishing you could take a sick day?

Different people have different ways of contributing to the world. And if you're not doing it in a way that's congruent with who you are, you'll end up unhappy. Maybe you're meant to contribute by creating art or entertaining people. Or perhaps you want to educate people. Only you know how you're supposed to add to the world around you.

Without a clear and compelling vision, you're just hanging

around aimlessly and hoping for the best! It's your job to upgrade your vision and stop pursuing half-baked goals that don't inspire you. You must decide to go after what you want and forget about the so-called 'realistic' goals you've been settling for.

Avoiding Regrets

> *'We must all suffer from one of two pains: the pain of discipline or the pain of regret. The difference is discipline weighs ounces while regret weighs tons.'*
>
> —Jim Rohn

If you were to die today, what regret(s) would you have? We tend to regret what we didn't do more so than what we did do. To borrow Wayne Dyer's words, the worst thing that can happen to you is 'dying with the music still in you.' It's leaving this world having betrayed yourself by living an inauthentic life driven by fear and excuses. It's leaving this world knowing that you could have done so much more. It means knowing that you wasted your time and potential doing unimportant things to impress people you didn't like and buy things you didn't need. It's leaving your projects unfinished because you didn't believe in yourself. It's never having had the courage to take the first step. It's having chosen comfort instead of growth, short-term gratification over long-term vision or hate over love.

Most people only scratch the surface of their real potential. They don't dig deep enough to reach the gold mine that lies within them. They'll look outside of themselves for answers that they can only find within. Jim Rohn used to say that success isn't something we should pursue, we should attract it by the person we become. I would say that success isn't something we should pursue. Instead, we should uncover it by finding out who we already are. After all, you can only be successful when your life is aligned with your core values.

Listening to Your Inner Voice

To improve your life, you must cut through the noise and go deep within. No one else can tell you what you should do, not society, not your family. Nobody will tell you to follow your passion, either. Most of the time, they'll dissuade you from doing so. Only you have the power to make your vision happen.

Nobody told me to create a website or write books. Nobody suggested that I quit my high-paying job to build an online business. I'd even bet that most of the people I know don't think I'll make it.

The same probably goes for you. As you choose to follow your passion, you'll start scaring the shit out of many people who, subconsciously, don't want you to succeed. Your success would make them question the choices they make, such as staying at an unfulfilling job or giving up on their dreams. If you fail, it will validate their decision to avoid risk and play it safe. It is for this reason that they have a vested interest in seeing you fail. It's nothing personal; it's just how the human mind works.

They'll often try to dissuade you by telling you that you have to be 'realistic.' Ignore them. Why would you listen to average people telling you to be realistic? Instead, start thinking and behaving like people who have what you want. Surround yourself with these people, either online or in real life by having mentors, coaches or friends that have already achieved the goals you're trying to reach.

Bear in mind that going the extra mile might mean you have to let go of some of the people in your life. That's the price of greatness.

Having Goals that Challenge You

The real value of your goals lies in what they require you to become to achieve them. If you already had all the qualities and skills needed, you would have reached your goals by now.

Your goals should be so big that you have to become an entirely different person to achieve them. They should scare you, but they should also inspire you to take action and go beyond your comfort zone.

Would you prefer to aim for the moon and land among the stars or pursue lackluster goals that don't inspire you?

Worthy goals should inspire you to become the best version of yourself. You can always grow more. And your goals are here to encourage you to do just that! The person you become in the process of achieving your most challenging goals will always be far more valuable than the goal itself. Imagine how much more persistent, disciplined, courageous, confident and resourceful you'll have to become to achieve your goals. Those are things that nobody can ever take away from you.

Don't Worry About the 'How'

Worrying about the 'how' is one of the most common mistakes people make when setting goals. The thing is, you don't need to know how you'll achieve your goals. Being aware of the first step you must take is enough. As you commit to taking that first step, the next one will come to you. Let your subconscious mind take care of the how while you take the first step.

The first step could be something as simple as:

- Making a phone call
- Buying a book
- Registering for a seminar
- Calling a friend
- Sending an email
- Doing research online
- Writing down your goal

As Confucius said, 'A journey of a thousand miles begins with a single step.' What is the first step that will start your thousand-mile journey?

The bottom line is this: forget about the 'how' and focus on the 'why' behind your goal instead. That 'why' is your vision. When your 'why' is powerful enough, it can help you move mountains and overcome any obstacle along the way.

Discovering Your 'Why'

It's easy to buy into society's definition of success and follow the herd. You may even have a successful career and make a lot of money, but if you're miserable, what's the point? What would you be doing if you stopped listening to your parents, friends or society and paid attention to your inner voice instead?

The reason your 'why' is so important is that it imbues everything you do with a sense of purpose and gives you meaning. When you hate your job, every task seems boring and meaningless. However, when you have a larger purpose, even trivial tasks become bearable or even mildly enjoyable. That's because your vision is like a magnet that pulls you. The pull of your vision is more powerful than the push from your boss. That's because you know that every task you work on, be it boring or exciting, is moving you closer to your vision.

In his book *The Entrepreneur Roller Coaster*, Darren Hardy admitted that he spends 95 per cent of his time doing things he doesn't enjoy. That's only possible because he has a compelling vision. I bet that if he had to do similar tasks at a tedious 9-5 job, it would be a real struggle for him.

What about you? What is your 'why' behind what you do?

Setting Crystal Clear Goals

Once you commit to your vision, the next step is to set crystal clear goals. We're naturally designed to solve problems and achieve goals. However, most people have only vague goals such as making more money, being successful or being happy. Unfortunately, unclear goals lead to mediocre results at best.

Every day, millions of people wake up as if by accident, wandering through life and hoping for the best. They have no clear goals in mind, no vision to go after, no purpose to actualize. You'd be surprised at how few people know what they want from life.

Your brain can't aim at a target that doesn't exist. Only when you have a distinct objective in mind can your brain operate at full capacity. That's why you have to spend most of your time focusing on what you want to achieve. You must focus your thoughts, actions and efforts on it. You must become obsessed.

Remember that a magnifying glass generates fire by directing the sun's rays to a specific point. Similarly, you create results by turning your focus towards a particular goal. Your concentration is your ultimate weapon.

Once you set a clear goal, your subconscious mind will start working on it 24/7; it'll look for ways to achieve your goals while you're sleeping. Under its influence, you'll be guided to take different actions. As you keep focusing on your goal and visualizing it, your emotional state will shift. That will impact your body language and vocal tone, which will cause those around you to react differently to you. While these things may be subtle, they'll affect your actions as well as the results you get.

Sadly, few people take advantage of their subconscious minds. Their goals are too vague, and their focus is unclear. Do you know what you want exactly? What does making more money, being successful or being happy mean to you? Can you visualize it?

Ideally, you should be able to visualize your goals as if they were memories. If you were wealthy would your memory be 'I made a lot of money this year'? No. It would be something very concrete that you can picture in your mind. Your memories would probably involve things like moving to a new house in a good neighborhood, traveling to specific countries or sending your kids to a fantastic school. You would have very detailed memories involving all five senses. Having more money would elicit a sense of pride or perhaps even freedom.

Note that a positive shift in your emotional state is a good sign that your visualization is effective. I seriously doubt that you want to make money just for the hell of it! It's what the money will give you that brings out the positive emotions.

Using the SMART Method

When you set goals, you want to make sure you use the SMART method.

SMART stands for:

- **S**pecific: What exactly do you want? What are you trying to achieve?
- **M**easurable: Can you easily assess your progress? How will you know you've reached your goal?
- **A**chievable: Is it achievable? Is the timeframe realistic? Can you put in the required effort despite your other responsibilities?
- **R**elevant: Is the goal aligned with your values? Does it excite you?
- **T**ime-bound: Do you have a clear deadline for your goal?

Chunking Down Your Goal

When you set your sights on a huge goal, it's easy to get discouraged. You can end up feeling overwhelmed and prone to self-sabotaging behaviors such as procrastination. You can avoid this by breaking your goal down into manageable tasks that you can work on every day. Any goal, no matter how big it is, can always be broken down into smaller tasks. In the next section, which discusses habits, you'll get a detailed look at how you can implement daily tasks that will help you achieve your goals.

What are some of the primary goals you'd like to accomplish in the coming years? How can you break them down into monthly, weekly and daily goals?

If you want to achieve a particularly challenging goal, *The One Goal*, my advanced goal-setting book, will help you master the goal-setting process and overcome mental blocks so that you can achieve your goal.

Your Daily Mantras:

Repeat the following mantras on a daily basis:

- I have absolute faith in my vision. If I can conceive it, I can and will, achieve it.
- I'm already there in my mind.

Action Step:

Spend a few minutes completing the corresponding exercise in the workbook (IV. Turbocharging your Vision)

6

IMPROVING YOUR INTEGRITY

On your deathbed, would you rather look back at your life knowing you stayed true to yourself or feel intense regret for having cheated the man in the glass?

Going the extra mile means living a life of integrity. By integrity I mean two things:

- **Honesty with yourself.** Living a life that aligns with your core values and knowing deep down that you're doing what you should.
- **Extreme honesty with other people.** Treating other people as you would like them to treat you

Being Honest with Yourself

Are you living your life according to your core values? Do you even know your core values? If what you're doing and who you are deep down don't match, you'll suffer the consequences.

Your core values are what matter most to you. It could be family values, freedom, growth, contribution, security or connection to name just a few. Let me give you some concrete examples:

- If your primary value is freedom and growth, then working 70–80 hours a week under a micro-managing

boss won't be fulfilling.
- If your most significant value is making connections, spending your work days in front of a computer and your nights watching TV won't make you happy.
- If your main value is making a contribution, and you aren't contributing to the world through your work, you'll be frustrated.
- If your biggest value is security, you might feel uncomfortable being an entrepreneur with all the uncertainty it entails.

It's vital to know yourself enough to live a life that reflects your values and personality. Are you an introvert or an extrovert? Do you know your Myer-Briggs type? What are your values? What are your strengths?

Some common personality tests are:

- DiSC Personality test
- Introvert / extrovert tests
- MBTI test
- VARK test
- The Big Five Personality Test

You'll find links to free versions of these tests, as well as additional resources, at the end of this book.

Being Honest with Others

Maintaining integrity in a world that can be unethical isn't easy. Marketing is one example of that: pushy salesmen that try to sell you things you don't want, copywriters who toy with you psychologically and commercials that promise you miraculous transformations. The examples are numerous. And don't get me started on how some politicians and corporations behave. We can't be living Buddhas, but we can strive to have as much integrity as possible.

Now, look at the situations below and see which choice you would make.

Situation 1:

The cashier at the supermarket makes a mistake when she gives you change.

1. You keep the money and don't say anything. She was dumb and made a mistake, so it's her problem.
2. You point out the issue and give her the extra change.

Situation 2:

You find a wallet with a lot of money in it.

1. You keep the money and the wallet or you keep the money and give the wallet back.
2. You give the wallet back, along with the money.

Many people would choose option one in both cases. I'm sure I know a person or two who would. Now, imagine that you're the cashier or the person who lost their wallet. Which option would you prefer? One or two?

We can always choose our attitude. Should the cashier have been more careful? Yes. Should the person who lost his or her wallet have been more careful? Probably. But does it give me the right to take the money? No. I didn't do anything to deserve that money.

Having integrity is not just about showing respect to other people, it's also about showing respect to yourself. There are many situations in which being dishonest seems inconsequential (like in the first situation with the change). Even in these scenarios, I'd prefer to do the right thing and feel good about it than receive benefits I don't deserve by doing the wrong thing.

Integrity, along with self-discipline, is what will earn you the trust of those around you. Imagine if your customers trusted you so much that they continually bought your products for years or even decades to come? Imagine if people trusted you so much that they couldn't wait to do business with you? How would things change for you?

In the long-term, integrity is a better strategy than cutting corners, as it will earn you the respect of others. And we know how crucial connections are, both in business and our personal lives. Sure, you can try to take shortcuts, but is that sustainable? And is that the legacy you want to leave? Do you want to be forever known as someone who took advantage of others to get ahead? You're worth more than that!

Your Daily Mantras:

Repeat the following mantras on a daily basis:

- I'm listening to my intuition and trusting my inner wisdom.
- I do what feels right to me, even if it's unpopular.
- What matters is what I do when nobody is watching.

Action Step:

Spend a few minutes completing the corresponding exercise in the workbook (VI. Improving your Integrity)

7

OPTIMIZING YOUR ENVIRONMENT

'You must be willing to destroy everything in your life that is not excellent.'

—Bo Eason

In his amazing book *The Success Principles*, Jack Canfield mentioned the story of Tim Ferris, the best-selling author of *The 4-Hour Work Week*. When he was 12- years-old, Ferris received an anonymous call that changed his life. The caller left the following quote from Jim Rohn on his answering machine: 'You are the average of the five people you spend the most time with.'

Ferris became obsessed with this quote. He realized that the kids he was hanging out with were having a negative impact on his life. Ferris knew that he would have to make changes in his life. That's when he asked his parents to send him to private school. That led to studying abroad in Japan where he discovered Judo and meditation. Later on, he entered Princeton University.

The rest, as they say, is history.

It's undeniable that our environment and the people we hang out with have a tremendous influence on us. The impact will be positive if we surround ourselves with highly optimistic and hard-working people. It will be detrimental if we surround ourselves with pessimistic and unambitious people.

Just a week ago, before going back to France, I was staying at my friend's place in Osaka, Japan. My friend, who is creating a company, works morning, noon and night, seven days a week. As you can imagine, this motivated me to work hard, too.

A few days later, I was staying at my brother's place in France. My brother has a lot of free time and spends most of it watching TV while playing games on his smartphone and tablet. I quickly noticed the impact this new environment had on my productivity and it wasn't a good one.

Our environment does matter! To improve your life, you must enhance your environment. As former professional football player Bo Eason says, 'You must be willing to destroy everything in your life that is not excellent.' Anything that's not helping you live the life you want is working against you. You should deal with everything that's limiting your potential. It means that you might have to cut off some of your friends or move to a new environment. Sometimes, that's the price you must pay to achieve the results you want.

Imagine if you only hung out with extraordinarily optimistic and highly successful friends, how would that affect you?

Your successful friends would have different habits than the average Joe. As you spend more time with them, you'd pick up on some of their behaviors. Your confidence would grow, you'd notice a positive influence on your work ethic and you'd start believing that your goals are possible. More importantly, you'd begin to adopt their mindset over time. And that's more valuable than having access to their potential network or their capital.

To adopt a more empowering mindset, what's better

than total immersion? As you see your friends doing things that you never thought possible, you start believing that you can do them, too. In short, you start realizing that you have more potential than you previously thought. That's why having mentors or coaches can also be extremely helpful: they embody what you want and know how to get it. That's also why almost every successful person has excellent mentors behind them.

Achieving meaningful goals is challenging enough; the last thing you want is to be around negative people who try to sabotage your efforts. What you want is to be around the best people you can find. If you can't meet these people in real life or don't have the money to hire a coach, go online and find successful people you can imitate.

Select a handful of people who have achieved the goals you want to reach and consume their content. Doing so will allow you to start absorbing their mindset. Look at their daily habits and implement similar ones in your life. As Tony Robbins says, 'If you want to be successful, find someone who has achieved the results you want and copy what they do and you'll achieve the same results.' Simple, isn't it?

What about you? What is the one thing you could do that would allow you to spend more time with positive, highly successful people? Will you start a program taught by someone you view as a role model? Join a group of like-minded people on Meetup? Hire a coach? Ask someone to be your mentor?

Remember, if you don't make a conscious effort to design your environment, negativity will find a way to creep in and make your surroundings less than optimal. Start destroying everything in your environment that is not excellent.

Your Daily Mantras:

Repeat the following mantras on a daily basis:

- I consciously create the ideal environment for growth and prosperity.
- I let go of people, places and objects that prevent me from living the life of my dreams.

Action Step:

Spend a few minutes completing the corresponding exercise in the workbook (VII. Optimizing your Environment)

8

SHARPENING YOUR SKILLS

'If people knew how hard I had to work to gain my mastery, it would not seem so wonderful at all.'

—Michelangelo

To get the results you want you must improve your skills until you reach a level of mastery. Fortunately, it's now easier than ever to learn a new skill or develop an existing one. With the Internet, we have access to all the information in the world. We can learn absolutely anything we want, often at little to no cost to us. We can buy millions of books on Amazon for a few bucks each, or watch billions of videos on YouTube for free. There's just no limit to what we can learn.

However, with so much information available, it's very easy to get lost, jumping from one thing to another without getting any tangible results. That's why you must commit to mastering a few critical skills and be honest enough to recognize what needs work.

So, how can you improve your current skills? What new skills do you need to develop to achieve your vision? Sometimes, despite all your efforts, you'll wind up stuck. Don't worry; we'll discuss how you can use deliberate practice to take your skills to a new level.

Adopting Deliberate Practice

They say that practice makes perfect, but is that true?

In this section, I'd like to talk about how you can break down skills into key tasks to enhance the quality of your practice and boost your results. You can work or practise as hard as you want, but if you do it mechanically without any strategy behind it, you're unlikely to get the results you want.

Practicing piano for 30 years won't automatically turn you into a world-class musician. Writing on a daily basis won't, in itself, turn you into the next Stephen King. Working hard isn't enough by itself. We must first get clear on what hard work is and isn't.

Did you know that doctors with decades of experience don't seem to provide better care to their patients than those with just a few years of experience? That's what researchers at Harvard Medical School found out as they reviewed research on changes in the quality of care provided by doctors over time. You would expect a doctor with decades of experience to be significantly more skilled than one who's just getting started, but that's not the case. The same goes for nurses, and I suspect that it applies to many other professions. Why is that?

Personally, I think it's because the more experienced doctors reach a plateau at some point and day-to-day work doesn't allow them to significantly improve their skills in a way that leads to higher quality care. They may be unaware of the ways they could provide better care. And, in many cases, they don't have access to the right training to help them improve their skills.

In the case of a rare disease, some doctors might find it challenging to come up with the right diagnosis. In this scenario, doctors would need precise training involving case studies and regular feedback. Other more passive types of training just won't do it. In fact, studies have shown that continuing education in the medical field, such as lectures and seminars, do little to help doctors improve their skills.

I would argue that, in most professions, people reach a plateau at some point. Unless they consciously decide to take their skills to a new level and engage in specific, deliberate practice to help them do so, they won't significantly improve their performance.

What is Deliberate Practice?

Deliberate practice is what differentiates someone who practises tennis for 15 years and becomes one of the top players from someone who plays tennis for 15 years as a hobby. While the first type of person keeps improving their game year after year, the second person only improves their game during the first few years of practice before getting stuck on a plateau for years on end.

If you aren't making tangible progress on your current goals, it's because you aren't applying deliberate practice. In fact, if you're anything like me, you've probably never used deliberate practice to improve your skills before. That, of course, leaves you with enormous room for improvement.

In their book *Peak, Secrets from The New Science of Expertise*, Anders Ericsson and Robert Pool define deliberate practice as follows:

- Deliberate practice builds skills for which effective training techniques have already been established.
- Deliberate practice takes place outside of your comfort

zone, requires significant effort and is generally not enjoyable.
- Deliberate practice involves specific, well-defined goals.
- Deliberate practice requires a person's full attention and conscious actions.
- Deliberate practice involves regular feedback that you give appropriate responses to.
- Deliberate practice both creates and relies on effective mental representation (the patterns we mentioned earlier).
- Deliberate practice almost always involves working on existing skills or building new ones by focusing specifically on some aspect of those skills that need to be improved.

It's not hard to imagine how the use of deliberate practice can lead to better long-term results than merely putting in 'hard work.' It allows you to work both smarter and harder by consciously focusing on improving the skills you need to reach your goal.

You might be thinking, 'If deliberate practice is so great, why aren't more people using it?' There are a few reasons for that.

First of all, the foundation of deliberate practice is existing training techniques that are effective. It works well with activities for which performance can be assessed like sports, playing instruments or chess. It's more challenging for other things where performance is harder to assess, such as teaching or business management.

Secondly, it requires effort. And let's face it, many people aren't willing to go through the hassle.

Thirdly, many people are unaware of deliberate practice

and how they can leverage it to improve their skills.

Below are some examples of what deliberate practice is and isn't.

Writing

Typical practice:

Writing, writing and more writing. In the words of Stephen King, 'If you want to be a writer, you must do two things above all others: read a lot and write a lot.' I don't doubt the importance of reading and writing more, but what if it's more complicated than that?

Deliberate practice:

Benjamin Franklin's story

It seems like Benjamin Franklin felt he needed to do more than reading and writing. He focused on improving specific skills: his writing style, vocabulary and sense of organization.

- Writing style: He made notes on articles from *Spectator*, a high-quality newspaper, which he would use to rewrite the articles a few days later. He would then compare his version to the original and modify it accordingly.
- Vocabulary: He rewrote *Spectator* essays in verse and then in prose so that he could compare his vocabulary to that which the original article used.
- Organization: He wrote summaries of every sentence in a particular article on separate sheets of paper. He would then wait a few weeks before challenging himself to write the article in the correct order and compare his work to the original article.

Doesn't that sound like fun? And he did that consistently while holding a full-time job!

Public Speaking

Typical practice:

Practicing a particular speech again and again until your performance becomes satisfactory.

Deliberate practice:

Focusing on a specific skill or aspect of your speech that would allow you to improve your overall performance. These skills include the following:

- The tone of your voice
- Your rhythm
- The structure of your speech
- Your body language/eye contact
- The use of your space
- How you tell stories
- Your vocal projection

Designing Your Deliberate Practice

The fastest and easiest way to use deliberate practice involves looking at what's already out there. There's no need to reinvent the wheel. How did the best in your field rise to the top? What are they doing on a daily basis? How do they train, how long do they train, and how often do they do it? To make the process easier, you can also hire a coach, find a mentor or buy programs that address your specific needs. That will help you reduce the learning curve and make faster progress.

There may not be a proven method you can rely on to help you achieve your goals. As such, you may need to create one on your own.

If so, the process below can be used to do just that.

- Break down the skills you must improve to achieve your goals
- Find out what aspects of each skill you must need to master
- Prioritize them in order of what's most important to master
- Find a way to work on these elements on a consistent basis (daily is best)
- Find a way to measure your progress

Let me give you a simple example of this.

Example 1: Let's say you're currently studying English and want to improve your listening skills. Now, we need to identify what aspects you need to work on to develop that specific skill.

Aspects:

Vocabulary: Perhaps you're having trouble understanding the language because your vocabulary needs growth.

Pronunciation: Maybe you know a lot of words, but you can't understand them in conversation because you don't know the correct pronunciation.

Speed: Maybe you feel like people are talking too fast and you don't have time to process their words.

Practice:

You could decide to watch a specific movie or video with subtitles until you can understand everything without them.

More specifically, you could block out 15–30 minutes of time each day to watch short videos on YouTube regarding a topic on which you'd like to work. Ideally, you'd start with short videos (one to two minutes).

- The first time around, you would listen to the videos and try to understand the words without looking at the subtitles.
- The second time, you would watch the video while looking at the subtitles.
- The third and fourth times, you would try to understand as much as you can without looking at the subtitles.
- The fifth and sixth times, you would watch the video while looking at the subtitles.
- Finally, you would write down the words you weren't already familiar with or that you couldn't quite catch.

You could also take some notes on how to improve your practice and reflect on any insights you may have. The next day, you would go through your vocabulary list and read it out loud. Then, you would repeat the process we just mentioned.

Once you understand everything, you could play the video at 1.5X or even 2X its original speed and repeat the process mentioned above. You could then repeat the process with more videos around the same topic, regularly going back to the videos you've previously watched to ensure you still understand them.

To measure your progress, you could select a specific video and use it as a benchmark. Ideally, it would cover a similar topic, and you would watch it just once according to a predetermined schedule (once a week or twice a month, for instance). Then, you would analyse how much you understood compared to the last time you saw it. You could even take it a step further by creating more specific criteria with which to evaluate yourself.

That would probably be how Benjamin Franklin would approach it. That's not as much fun as watching an entire movie with subtitles while eating ice-cream, right? No one said the path to mastery was easy!

How could you design a specific training regimen that would allow you to get better results with your goals?

Your Daily Mantras:

Repeat the following mantras on a daily basis:

- I love improving my skills every day. I'm becoming so good that others are starting to notice.
- I know beyond a shadow of a doubt that I can learn anything I set my mind to.

Action Step:

Spend a few minutes completing the corresponding exercise in the workbook (VIII. Sharpening your Skills)

9

UPGRADING YOUR HABITS

'It's what you do every day that counts. Eating 7 apples on Sunday won't keep the doctor away'.

It's what you do every day, not what you do sporadically, that will determine the results you get in life.

Going the extra mile with your habits means that you commit to implementing a few core habits that you'll do every single day for years to come. These core habits compound over time and will help you achieve the results you want. Don't underestimate the power of small habits. Even seemingly trivial habits will yield incredible results when you follow through consistently over an extended period.

For instance, one of my small habits is to write 500 words every day, no exceptions. While that may not sound much, that's more than 180,000 words per year. Or, in other words, eight 25,000-word books like this one over the course of 12 months. That's 40 books after five years, and 160 books after 20 years. And that's assuming I only write 500 words per day. I usually write more than that.

Other small habits like daily meditation or daily gratitude exercises will significantly increase your well-being. The good news is that you can start with just a few minutes a day. Isn't it worth investing a few minutes of your time?

For a detailed step-by-step method for implementing lifelong habits, refer to my book *Habits That Stick: The Ultimate Guide To Building Powerful Habits That Stick Once And For All.*

If you want to step up your game, having consistent daily habits is an absolute necessity. 'Consistent' is the big word here. In the long run, consistency will yield exceptional results. If you aren't convinced, take a look at the main benefits of daily habits, which I've listed below.

- **Daily habits are harder to skip**: when you commit to a daily habit, you remove all excuses. With a habit that you perform a few times a week, you can always come up with excuses and skip it once in a while. No big deal, right? Wrong. Skipping makes you lose momentum. A few weeks later, your new habit is gone forever.
- **Daily habits help you build momentum**: daily habits are great to build momentum and maintain it. You skip your habit once, lose momentum, and give up. We've all been there. As you learn to stay consistent with your daily habits, you'll continually build momentum and your motivation will remain high.
- **Daily habits help you build self-discipline**: A daily habit is a simple commitment that you make to yourself every day. When you decide to do something daily, regardless of what it is, it improves your self-discipline. Discipline is like a muscle; the more you use it, the stronger it becomes. That's probably one of the reasons soldiers are asked to make their beds every day.

How to Create Daily Habits

When it comes to implementing new habits, people tend to be overly ambitious. They think that setting huge goals every day will help them make drastic changes in their lives at a faster rate than they otherwise would.

Unfortunately, that's usually counter-productive. Few people have enough discipline to make drastic changes in a short period. It's far better to think of your goals as a marathon, rather than a sprint.

Anything worthwhile takes time (and usually significantly more time than you think). Small daily habits are far less challenging to sustain long-term. They also allow you to do the following:

- **Avoid procrastination.** We're all tempted to procrastinate from time to time. When your habit is so small that it requires minimal effort, you're less likely to put it off. Running for three minutes per day doesn't sound that difficult. Writing 50 words a day isn't a daunting task. Doing one pushup? A piece of cake!
- **Build momentum.** As you stay consistent with your habit, you'll build momentum and feel motivated to do more. While your small habit may be to run for three minutes, you may end up running 30 minutes after a few weeks. Or you could end up writing 2,000 words per day when your minimum target is 50.
- **Feel good about yourself.** As you stick to your habits day after day, you'll start feeling good about yourself and your self-esteem will grow.

Defining Your Daily Core Tasks

There are always a few core tasks that, if focused on each day, will allow you to achieve your goals over time. Daily habits (your core tasks) are an efficient way to ensure that you move one step closer to your goals every day.

Sticking to them shouldn't be too much trouble. After all, if you can't spare a small portion of your day to work on your goals, then are they genuinely that important to you?

In my case, one of my core tasks is to write. As I mentioned previously, I make sure I write at least 500 words every single day. Ideally, I want to maintain that habit for many years to come.

The first key point is to identify the core tasks that will allow you to achieve your goal. The second is to do something regarding that task every single day. Sounds simple, right?

I'm still working on identifying these core tasks myself. Since my primary focus is writing books and blog posts, writing is one of my core tasks. I must write every single day. Apart from writing, I'm also considering implementing an editing habit or another exercise that would help me improve my writing.

The second core task I identified is marketing. Without effective marketing, I'll remain unknown and will be unable to bring in enough revenue to support myself. I have to define my daily core tasks and create a specific schedule around marketing. One idea is dedicating a block of time to marketing activities every day (Facebook marketing, YouTube marketing, search engine optimization, landing pages, etc.)

Another area I want to work on is public speaking. In addition to recording videos and doing Facebook Live, I want to create video courses. For that purpose, it's essential that I work on improving my speaking skills. However, I have yet to define a specific daily core task for that.

Two or three core tasks performed daily will ensure that you stay on track with your goals and maintain momentum over time. Make sure you use the principles outlined in the section on deliberate practice to design your core tasks. It will yield excellent results over time.

Finally, remember that the journey is a marathon, not a sprint.

Your Daily Mantras:

Repeat the following mantras on a daily basis:

- I'm proud of being the most consistent person I know.
- Every day I'm moving closer to my goal.
- I know that it's what I do every day that's creating my future.

Action Step:

Spend a few minutes completing the corresponding exercise in the workbook (IX. Upgrading your Habits)

10

BOOSTING YOUR PRODUCTIVITY

'Lack of direction, not lack of time, is the problem. We all have twenty-four hour days.'

—Zig Ziglar

Productivity and time management are essential skills for people who want to get better results in life. Most people undervalue their time. They behave as if money were more important than time and would gladly trade it to save money.

On the other hand, genuinely productive people understand that time is more important than money. They know that they can always make more money, but they can never get more time. They're the ones who would gladly spend money to save time.

If you want to know how productive you are, look at the way you use your time. Do you spend hours looking for the best deal online so that you can save a few dollars? Is that something a wealthy person would do? Probably not. They consider their time so valuable that they wouldn't bother doing tasks that they can easily outsource to other people. It didn't happen overnight, but over time they learned to outsource or delegate low-value tasks to focus on more productive ones. You can learn to do this, too.

Remember that you can always recoup money, but you can never get your time back. Every second that passes is gone forever, and nothing in the world can change that.

Defining Productivity

What is your definition of productivity? For instance, would you say that someone who makes six figures working 70 hours at a job they hate is productive? That person might be the company's most productive employee, but is that what productivity is all about?

For me, productivity doesn't necessarily mean making a lot of money for each hour I work. Instead, **it means spending most of my time doing what I love**. That's making good use of your time. And isn't that what productivity is about?

I sometimes go for 30 to 60 minute walks, which I love. Considering I'm building a business, you may think I'd be better off spending that time working. That's not how I see it. Walking is something I sincerely enjoy. Therefore, how could it not be a good use of my time?

Going for a walk is also a great way to refresh my mind. In fact, my best ideas often come when I'm walking, not when I'm sitting at my desk thinking as hard as I can.

What about you? What is your definition of productivity?

Action Step:

Use the workbook to write down your definition of productivity.

The Importance of Task Management

I prefer the term task management over time management. That's because we can't manage time. Time is entirely beyond our control. We can, however, control what we do during the time we have. When you start thinking about task management, it becomes easier to set an effective strategy for productivity.

Productivity Made Simple

You don't need to implement complicated systems to boost your productivity. When it comes to productivity, simpler is better. The endless search for the perfect productivity tool is often a distraction or an excuse to avoid getting the job done. To paraphrase Brian Tracy, you have to train yourself to eat that disgusting frog every day. There's no other way around it.

Because you refuse to eat that metaphorical frog, you look for a magical productivity tool that, you hope, will revolutionize your productivity. It may help you, but you have to master the fundamentals first!

An Effective Yet Simple Productivity Method

Forget about complex tools. Here's how to increase your productivity in one sentence:

Every morning, write down three to six tasks that would ensure you have the most productive day possible, start working on the most critical one (usually the thing you want to do last), complete it, move to the next task and repeat.

That's it!

Completing a few important tasks is more rewarding than

wrestling with an ever-increasing to-do list. It also prevents you from believing you're productive when you aren't. Ticking off items on a random to-do list might feel good, but you're just prolonging the life of your frog if the tasks are trivial.

Even so, I encourage you to create a to-do list on a separate piece of paper. You can then handpick your most significant tasks from that list.

This system works for both weekly and monthly goals. In fact, most of your daily goals come from breaking down your weekly, monthly or yearly goals. At the beginning of each month, schedule time in your calendar to write down your monthly goals. Then, select three to six essential tasks or projects you want to complete. If you do this each week, you'll be amazed at the results.

While there is a little bit more to productivity than what I've just said, that's the gist of it. It's simple, but you'd be surprised at how few people use this system. Don't let the simplicity fool you, however. Get rid of any expectations you have of getting it right the first time. It may be simple, but you'll still have to get adjusted to it. You'll have to repeat the process every day until you start grabbing your notes and writing your tasks down automatically. The key here is consistency.

In *The Ultimate Sales Machines*, Chet Holmes revealed that he had looked over the shoulders of his employees for months before they started using his system consistently.

The first step to becoming one of the most productive people you know is to write down your most important tasks every day and then do your best to complete them. Implement this strategy every day until you master it. Then, and only then, should you look for tools to help you further boost your productivity.

Planning for Interruptions

The number of interruptions you'll face at work will vary from job to job, but either way, you're going to have to deal with them. They may come in the form of people asking for your help, a large number of phone calls, lots of emails or dozens of items you receive in the mail each day. To allow enough time for your daily duties, Chet Holmes recommends a maximum completion time of six hours for your tasks.

Planning Your Day in Advance

To boost your productivity, learn to plan your day the night before. That's helpful for two main reasons:

1. It will prime your subconscious mind. As you plan your day, your subconscious mind will start working on your tasks. It might generate new ideas, inspire you, or even come up with solutions during your sleep.
2. It will leave you ready to work right away and avoid procrastination. As you prepare everything you need to complete your tasks, you'll be prepared to work first thing in the morning, which reduces the risk of procrastination.

Note that a lack of clarity is what often leads us to procrastinate.

A Crash Course in Crushing Procrastination

How often do you feel the urge to grab a coffee, go on YouTube, or check Facebook as you're about to tackle a new task? If you're like most people, you get this urge frequently. Let me give you three simple steps to overcome procrastination and eat that damned frog.

1. Become aware of your procrastination.

The first step to overcoming procrastination is to become mindful. When the urge to procrastinate kicks in, what thoughts do you have? What feelings arise?

We all have different ways of procrastinating. As you observe your feelings, you'll uncover how you procrastinate. Do you feel the urge to watch TV? Do you want to go for a walk? Do you experience specific negative thoughts that sabotage your efforts?

Noticing these feelings will help you overcome procrastination.

2. Stay with your emotions.

The second step is staying with the feelings that arise as you're working on a task. We usually procrastinate for the reasons listed below.

Fear of failure:

We often procrastinate because we're afraid we won't do a good job. That makes sense, doesn't it? We think 'What if what I'm working on sucks?' and 'I don't think I'm good enough to do this well.'

Lack of clarity regarding what we need to do:

Another situation that may lead to procrastination is poorly defined tasks. Not knowing what to do leaves ample room for our mind to distract and sabotage us. That's how you end up watching cat videos on YouTube.

The desire to avoid pain and seek pleasure:

As human beings, we try to maximize enjoyment and prevent pain. Thus, we tend to resist any activity that we identify as 'painful.' Seeing painful tasks as a path toward a desirable outcome or as a part of a compelling vision can help us overcome the urge to procrastinate.

Lack of self-discipline:

Often, we merely lack self-discipline. Poor self-discipline is usually due to a diminished understanding of how our mind works: we over-identify with our brain and buy into the load of excuses it creates.

Fortunately, we are not our mind. Though our brain may try hard to convince us to procrastinate, ultimately, we can choose to ignore it. That's what self-discipline is. In the corresponding section, we'll discuss self-discipline in greater detail.

Lack of commitment:

Many people lack commitment and happily say 'yes' to everything before ultimately failing to deliver on what they agreed to. The more you keep your promises to yourself and others, the easier it will be for you to complete your tasks.

Perfectionism:

Another issue is the desire to be perfect. While the desire to do great work is understandable, completing something 80 per cent is a far better than aiming for 99 per cent. It results in a massive productivity boost and offers additional opportunities for improvement. Where you would have previously spent countless hours perfecting minor details, you can now produce more and improve the process. Long-term, you'll end up becoming more productive while creating higher quality work.

3. Get started anyway:

Now that you have a better understanding of why you procrastinate, it's time to move on to the third step: getting started.

Define what you need to do:

Before you tackle a task, make sure you know what you need to do. Ask yourself, 'What specifically do I need to do here?' The clearer you can be, the less you'll procrastinate.

Remind yourself that you're not your mind's 'bitch':

Most people are slaves to their brain, but it should be the other way around. Your brain is a tool to help you achieve your goal, not a master that dictates your actions.

Feeling tired doesn't mean that you should procrastinate. Your mind may send you a signal that it's tired, but you can still push through it and get the task done. You can choose to overrule your mind!

Navy SEAL David Goggins lives by the 40 per cent rule. Having run ultra-marathons and pushed himself in many ways, he knows his stuff. The 40 per cent rule states that, when you believe you can't take it anymore, you still have a lot of energy left. Think about it. Doesn't it make sense that your brain would store energy to ensure you survive in case of an emergency?

The bottom-line is that working on your side business for a few hours after work when you feel tired won't kill you. You can do more than you think, but you'll never know that unless you train your mind.

Start small to release pressure:

The task in front of you might seem daunting. However, when you decide to give it a shot for five or 10 minutes, it suddenly seems less challenging. Setting a specific target to aim for can also help. For instance, one of my daily goals is to write 500 words a day. Because it's a rather easy target, I'm less prone to procrastination, and often end up writing more than 500 words. After working a few minutes on a task, you'll usually find yourself in the flow, which can lead to working on something for hours on end.

Permit yourself to suck:

Do you believe that the quality of your work won't be good enough? If so, permit yourself to suck! If you suck today, you'll suck tomorrow or next week. What magical thing will increase your ability to churn out fantastic work if you think you suck right now? Procrastinating won't solve that problem. Suck at it if you will, but just get started.

Remove all distractions:

Make sure you remove all distractions from your work environment. When I work, I like to remove everything from my desk. No phone, no food, no nothing. I'm sure I don't need to remind you to exit Facebook and other social media sites. Removing everything from your desk sends a signal to your mind that says 'I'm working now.'

Make things as easy as possible:

Your mind can quickly get distracted and come up with thousands of excuses to avoid doing real work. Don't make its job any easier. Follow the tips below instead.

- Make sure that everything you need is instantly accessible. That will make completing your task feel like a natural thing to do.
- Whenever you can, set your goals the day before and start visualizing yourself going through your tasks one after the other.
- Remove any obstacles you can think of. If, for example, you're a writer, think of what you're going to write about the day before or leave a chapter unfinished so that you know where to start. It will help you get into the groove quickly.

Your Daily Mantras:

Repeat the following mantras on a daily basis:

- It feels good to be the most productive person I know.
- I love how efficiently I'm using my time to create the life I want.
- I'm valuing my time because I'm valuing myself.

Action Step:

Spend a few minutes completing the corresponding exercise in the workbook (X. Boosting your Productivity)

11

ENHANCING SELF-DISCIPLINE

'Self-discipline is the ability to do what you should do, when you should do it, whether you feel like it or not.'

—Elbert Hubbard

There are a lot of misconceptions regarding self-discipline. In this section, I'll invite you to redefine your relationship with self-discipline so that you can achieve higher levels of success. My objective is to inspire you to go the extra mile and become the most disciplined person you know.

If you're like most people, you probably don't like the term 'self-discipline.' It evokes thoughts of pain and discomfort, and you would rather spend time with your friends or watching TV. However, self-discipline is beneficial in many ways, some of which you may not even be aware of. Self-discipline is very empowering.

Below are the main benefits that come with enhancing your self-discipline.

1. Self-discipline Creates Freedom

First of all, self-discipline is the basis for freedom. Without self-discipline, you can't enjoy real freedom. For a better understanding of what I mean, think about the points listed below.

- How can you be free if you have no control over your body, mind and actions? Where is the freedom in that?
- How can you be free if you're continually depressed and have no control over your emotions?
- How can you be free when you can't discipline yourself to do what's necessary to live the life you want?

I'd like you to start seeing self-discipline as your path to more freedom. Who doesn't want more freedom? When I think of self-discipline, I think of all the freedom that self-discipline can offer me. Because freedom is my most important value, I understand that I must cultivate more self-discipline to create more of it in my life.

When I was an employee, I worked on my online business in the morning before work and at night after work. Guess what? Though I'm passionate about what I do, I wasn't always thrilled to work on my business after a full day of work. Still, I did it every time, because I understood that it was the only way to create the freedom I wanted and design the life of my dreams.

After I quit my job a few months ago and no longer had a boss telling me what to do, I realized even more how crucial self-discipline was to a life of freedom. If I can't discipline myself to do what I need to do, I'll have to go back to a regular 9–5 job, which isn't an option for me.

In fact, I believe that lack of discipline is one of the main reasons people choose to have 9–5 jobs. Here is a crucial question if you're considering self-employment: are you confident that you can discipline yourself more efficiently than your boss?

I also realized that, without a clear structure and the self-discipline to enforce it on a daily basis, I would end up unhappy or even depressed. When we seek out increased freedom, we need a structure to express it in.

You may believe that having total freedom would make you happy. You may think you'll be in paradise once you've accumulated enough wealth to retire. Unfortunately, that's not true. It is, for the most part, a myth. Without boundaries and a clear structure, most people will become depressed no matter how wealthy they are.

Now, imagine if you had absolute control over your mind and body. Imagine if procrastination wasn't an issue. Imagine if you were confident that you'd do what you say you will. How much more could you accomplish? How much more likely would you be to achieve your most exciting goals?

Self-discipline is the path toward freedom: the freedom to control your body, mind and actions. This control results in the freedom to create the life you want.

2. Self-discipline Builds Trust

Another benefit of self-discipline is that it turns you into an extremely reliable person. People know that whatever you say you'll do will get done. That causes your friends, colleagues or customers to start trusting you more and will make more people want to work with you.

When you look at the most successful people around you, you'll notice that they're the ones with the most self-discipline. If you ask them to do something, you know they'll get the job done.

You can test this out for yourself. Look around you. Of all the people you know, how many do what they said say they'll do 99.9 per cent of the time? If you were to ask someone for a favor and had to bet your life on their ability to follow through, who would you ask? Chances are, the person you would choose has plenty of self-discipline.

3. Self-discipline Boosts Your Self-esteem

Finally, developing your self-discipline boosts your self-esteem. Few people realize the direct connection between self-discipline and self-esteem, but how can you respect yourself if you never do what you say you'll do?

4. Self-discipline Strengthens Your Ability to Achieve Your Goals

Another obvious benefit of self-discipline is that it strengthens your ability to achieve your goals. The more you can discipline yourself to accomplish your tasks each day, the more confident you'll become that you can reach your long-term goals.

How to Develop Extreme Self-discipline

Now, I'd like to give you a few simple tips to help you go the extra mile with your self-discipline. If you want to develop extremely high levels of self-discipline it's essential that you stop breaking promises to yourself and others. We're going to talk about how you can do that, but first, let me explain what I mean by breaking promises.

Breaking promises to yourself:

Each time you tell yourself you'll do something but don't, your self-esteem suffers. If you do it repeatedly, the empty promises you make to yourself lose their power. If you know that whatever you promise won't get done, what's the point in making promises to yourself? Breaking promises to yourself will ultimately cause you to stop setting goals.

Breaking promises to others:

When you say 'yes' to something but don't do what you said you'd do, people around you start seeing you as unreliable and become reluctant to work with you.

5 Tips to Become an Incredibly Disciplined Person

To turn yourself into an incredibly disciplined person, you must learn to keep your promises no matter what. There is no such thing as 100 per cent consistency, but you should at least aim for 99 per cent.

Below are some examples of what I mean by being disciplined:

1. **Always be on time.** If you can't show up on time, you're wasting other people's time. And time is the most precious resource we have. We can never get it back once it's gone. How can people trust you if you can't even respect their time? Showing up on time is the least you can do.
2. **Always show up.** If you're invited to an event and accepted the invitation, then show up! People should know that once you say yes, you'll be there no matter what.
3. **Finish what you start.** Discipline yourself to finish what

you start. It will significantly improve your productivity. Don't complete something 75 per cent or even 99 per cent, finish it 100 per cent as often as possible. That prevents you from losing momentum and having to go back to the same task twice. It requires time to develop this habit, but it will serve you well in the future. Fortunately, self-discipline is like a muscle. The more you discipline yourself to finish something, the better you'll become at it. Start by completing small tasks while avoiding distractions.
4. **Keep your promises.** Make sure that each time you agree to do something, you deliver on your promise. If you're unsure about your ability to do something, say 'no,' or 'maybe.' Don't commit to things unless you know you'll get them done.
5. **Start with the small stuff.** How you do one thing is how you do everything. If you can't even do simple things right, you'll have difficulties keeping more substantial commitments. In the army, soldiers have to make their beds every single morning. I believe that one of the reasons for this is to increase self-discipline and consistency. Be like a soldier. Make sure you have specific daily habits that you do consistently. For instance, I have a daily morning ritual, and I make sure that I meditate and set my goals every day. As a result, I've built more self-discipline. What about you?

If you implement the five tips mentioned above and go the extra mile, you'll become one of the most reliable people you know, and you'll stand out among a sea of flaky people.

Don't worry about being perfect, though. I'm still working on building stronger self-discipline myself, but I aim to become the most reliable person I know.

Remember, self-discipline is your ability to do things when you don't feel like it. That's what makes the difference between average people and highly successful people. That's also what will allow you to create the life you want and enjoy the level of freedom to which you aspire. Pretty cool, isn't it?

Your Daily Mantras:

Repeat the following mantras on a daily basis:

- I love being self-disciplined. The more discipline I am, the more freedom I'm creating in my life.
- I pride myself on finishing everything I start.
- I enjoy delivering on everything I commit to.

Action Step:

Spend a few minutes completing the corresponding exercise in the workbook (XI. Enhancing your Self-discipline)

12

TAKING CARE OF YOUR HEALTH

'Health is like money, as long as you have it, you don't think about it; when you lose it, you can't stop thinking about it.'

What I'm going to say in this chapter are things that you already know, but they're worth repeating. How could I not mention health in a book that encourages you to go the extra mile and become your best self?

Your health is probably one of the things you take for granted the most. But it's the most important thing! Ironically, you don't realize how important it is until you lose it.

Health problems affect every area of your life. They impact your energy levels, mood and ability to enjoy life. Thus, your health is the most important investment you can make. Who wants to get sick just after retirement?

Despite this, few people invest in their health to the extent that they should. Most of us treat both our mental and physical health as if they weren't particularly relevant. In 1900, American households spent close to half of their total budget on food (43 per cent). In 2003, food accounted for a mere 13 per cent of household budgets. People are willing to spend hundreds of dollars to buy the latest iPhone, but they can't even bother to buy proper food because they 'don't have enough money.' That's because they don't see their health as something in which to invest. How can you not have money to take care of your health?! If you think investing in your health is expensive, try being sick and see what happens. That's going to cost you a whole lot more money, not to mention the pain that comes with it.

Many diseases can be prevented by a healthy diet and proper exercise. Sadly, most of the food sold in the supermarket nowadays is crap. Even the nutritional value of fruits and vegetables has decreased over the past few decades.

I remember seeing a documentary about the food given in American schools. In some schools, they served fast food every day. The ridiculous thing was that pizzas are considered vegetables because of the tomato sauce that comes on them. Apparently, French fries are vegetables too, now! What a joke!

The fact is that society doesn't want you to be healthy. Big corporations can make much more money when you're sick than when you're healthy. As long as food and pharmaceutical companies make money, everything is fine.

If you don't take responsibility for your health, you're in trouble, because nobody else will. Only you can choose what you put in your mouth.

Keeping the Big Picture in Mind

Nutrition is a complex topic: eggs are the healthiest food on earth today, tomorrow they're unhealthy. One study finds that coffee is beneficial to you, another warns against drinking too much of it. Not to mention lobbyist groups that do whatever they can to sell their products whether they benefit us or not.

Under these conditions, no wonder people are confused. To avoid getting lost, let's keep the big picture in mind. Fortunately, eating healthy doesn't have to be rocket science.

A Few General Rules to Know

Regardless of how complicated nutrition can be, there are some simple guidelines that, if followed, will help us remain healthy.

1. You are what you eat

Pharmaceutical companies don't promote this fact because it's not in their interest to have a nation of healthy people, but you are what you eat. What you eat has a profound impact on your health. Your energy comes from what you eat, so it's only natural that the food you consume profoundly impacts your health.

For instance, few people know that you can cure type 2 diabetes with a healthy diet. Even fewer people know the incredible effect of plant-based foods on people who have heart disease. For instance, three-quarters of the patients who followed a program for reversing heart disease experienced marked and long-lasting reduction in angina—without surgery. The program, which was developed by Dean Ornish, M.D., contains five main components:

1. A very low-fat, whole foods, vegetarian (near-vegan) diet
2. 30 minutes of daily exercising (walking, etc.)
3. 30 minutes of daily stretching, meditation, relaxation, stress reduction activities, etc.
4. Psychological and emotional support groups
5. No smoking

That's the power of food and lifestyle changes!

Three main components affect our health: the food we eat, the thoughts and emotions we have and the environment in which we live. Thus, a healthy diet, a positive mindset and a healthy environment can go a long way in preventing diseases. While we shouldn't forget about our genes, they don't play as big of a role as we may think.

For instance, in cases of heart disease, heredity is rarely the cause of the disease. In the words of cardiac surgeon Michael Debby, 'It's true that a small percentage of patients have a hereditary form of arteriosclerosis in the sense that in their immediate family and their parents' and grandparents' families, there is a high incidence of atherosclerosis and coronary heart disease... But that only constitutes about five per cent of the cases. Most people (who develop heart disease) don't really have a hereditary disease.'

2. Whole, real, unprocessed food is almost always healthy

In an article published on the Forbes website, Johny Bowden (author of *The 150 Healthiest Foods on Earth*) wrote, 'Whole, real, unprocessed food is almost always healthy, regardless of how many grams of carbs, protein, or fat it contains.' If you avoid eating processed food alone, you'll already be on your way to improving your health. The more you buy unprocessed food and cook yourself, the better. Processed food includes anything that comes in a package (cookies, ready-to-eat meals, etc.) as well as food that includes refined sugar and flour such as pasta, rice and bread.

3. There are no bad vegetables

Experts disagree on all kind of things, but if there's one thing that leaves little room for controversy, it's the health benefits of veggies. It's unlikely that you'll hear a warning you that you're eating too many vegetables! In the words of Johny Bowden, 'The more plant foods, the better.'

4. Fruits are typically good for your health

Generally speaking, fruits are good for your health. If you have diabetes or other diseases, however, you may have to avoid certain fruits or reduce your daily intake of them. Choose raw fruits or fruit juices made from fresh fruits. The fruit juice you buy at the grocery store isn't healthy. It's just sugar. Don't be fooled.

5. The less refined sugar, the better

Refined sugar is empty calories. It's detrimental to your health and has no particular upside. 'Added sugars either crowd out healthy foods, or they make you fat if you eat them in addition to healthy foods,' explains Frank Sacks, a professor of cardiovascular disease prevention at the Harvard School of Public Health in Boston. Also, remember that your brain sees sugar as a reward. The more sugar you eat, the more you reinforce that reward. So start cutting down on the amount of sugar in your diet.

6. Many foods advertised as healthy aren't that healthy

Some foods advertised as healthy are anything but. That includes fat-free products, sugar-free products and many so-called 'natural' products. Even the benefits of 'organic' foods are dubious, as the definition of the word 'organic' is often blurred. Make sure you do your research.

To Sum it Up

I'm a not a nutritionist, so take my words with a grain of salt and do your research. My basic advice is to avoid processed foods and cook for yourself as much as possible. That way you know what's in your meals. Most processed food contains way too much sugar or salt along with who knows what. As we've seen previously, eating vegetables and fruits, reducing carbs (bread, rice, pasta, etc.) and staying away from sugar is probably a good idea as well. These are the things upon which most experts will agree. Apart from that, you'll find different people saying different things so, again, do your research. It's your health, not anybody else's!

Some Common Traps to Avoid

Often, we wrongly believe that certain foods are healthy. Then, when we fail to see any weight loss or improvement in our well-being, we get distressed. Below are some traps to be aware of:

A Vegetarian Diet is Not Necessarily a Healthy Diet

If you're a vegetarian, but eat mostly potato chips, bread, pasta and cookies, your diet is not healthy! If you chose to become vegetarian for health reasons, you'd be better off eating quality meat substitutes along with vegetables.

Do Your Research with Dietary Supplements

While supplements may help you get all of the vitamins and minerals you need, the effectiveness of many of them is questionable. Some supplements can help you if you have a deficiency, but others will be useless or even harmful. Not all supplements are made equal. Your body will be better able to absorb high-quality supplements, which makes them more efficient than run-of-the-mill vitamins.

Do Your Research Before Purchasing Dietary Supplements

More importantly, avoid buying vitamins if you can get them in your food (and you generally can).

Calories Aren't Everything

When trying to lose weight, many people get overly focused on their daily calorie intake. While eating fewer calories will help you lose weight, it doesn't guarantee that you're eating healthy. It all depends on what's in the calories you eat.

A Perfect Ratio of Protein, Carbs, and Fats is not what Matters Most

Again, coming up with the ideal ratio of protein, carbs and fats (if that even exists) doesn't guarantee that you're eating healthy. As Johny Bowden explained, '...the actual quality of the food we eat is probably way more important for our health than the proportions of fat, carbs, and protein.'

4 Critical Factors for Your Health

In his book *The 150 Healthiest Foods on Earth*, Johnny Bowden identifies four key factors to bear in mind when looking for healthy foods:

Omega 3

'It's been estimated by Andrew Still, M.D., of Harvard Medical School that proper omega-3 intake could save 70,000 lives a year in the United States alone and reduce the number of fatal arrhythmias by 30 per cent. Omega-3s help lower blood pressure. And they're also very effective for diabetics in improving insulin and glucose metabolism.' –Johny Bowden

Fibers

According to Johny Bowden, 'a high-fiber diet will probably reduce the risk of developing type 2 diabetes.' It's also 'the number-one supplement for weight loss' since high-fiber foods tend to 'fill you up longer.'

Glycemic Index

The glycemic index indicates how much a given food raises our blood sugar. That's important because food with a high glycemic index raises the level of insulin. When our insulin is raised high enough for long enough, it contributes to diabetes, heart disease, and aging.

Antioxidants

Antioxidants play an important role in keeping us healthy. Johny Bowden wrote that 'deficiencies of antioxidants are implicated in the early stages of heart disease, cancer, eye disease and age-related declines in memory.'

List of Healthy Products

Harvard Medical School recommends eating more of the following:

Fruits and vegetables, whole grains, fish and seafood, vegetable oils, beans, nuts and seeds.

While eating less of:

Whole milk and other full-fat dairy foods, red meat, processed meats, highly refined and processed grains and sugars and sugary drinks.

You'll find a longer list of some of the healthiest products on earth at the end of this book.

Exercising

Exercise plays an essential role in keeping us healthy. You don't have to run 10 miles every day to reap the benefits of exercising.

For instance, something as simple as walking 30 minutes, five days a week will have a positive long-term impact on your health. Research published in PLoS Medicine that included more than 650,000 people showed that 150 minutes of moderate exercise a week could add 3.4 years to your life.

Another study that included 5,000 Danes showed that regular exercisers live five to seven years longer than inactive people.

Exercising is not only beneficial for your health, but it's also great for your cognitive abilities. Your brain needs physical activity to function at its best, so make sure you take great care of your health.

What activity are you going to take on to further improve your health?

Your Daily Mantras:

Repeat the following mantras on a daily basis:

- My body is my temple. I love eating foods that celebrate my body.
- I love eating healthy food that gives me the energy and vitality to achieve my goals.

Action Step:

Spend a few minutes completing the corresponding exercise in the workbook (XII. Taking Care of your Health)

13

MASTERING YOUR EMOTIONS

'There is nothing good or bad, but thinking makes it so.'

—Shakespeare

Emotions are one of the most potent tools for your personal growth: they tell you whether you're on the right track. Because of this, learning to master your emotions is a must.

As you work on raising your standards, you'll face self-doubt, fear, frustration, disappointment, exhaustion and even existential crises. Your ability to understand your emotions and use them to your advantage will largely determine whether you'll achieve your goals.

Too many people have failed due to lack of control regarding their emotions. Sadly, self-doubt and fear have killed more dreams than anything else in the world. Don't let your negative feelings kill your dreams.

Distancing Yourself from Your Emotions

The most important thing to understand is that you are not your emotions. The only thing that gives power to your feelings is the attention you give them. An emotion that you don't pay attention to will quickly fade away. The same goes for your thoughts. In fact, your feelings arise from thoughts or beliefs. When you identify with them, it triggers a specific emotion and as you bring your attention to it, it becomes stronger and stronger.

That's why you sometimes see people holding grudges for insignificant events that happened years ago. They focused on the emotion as it arose and kept focusing on it again and again to the point where it left a footprint in their mind. Had they let go of the emotion as it arose, it would have died out a long time ago.

I have a specific way of avoiding situations like this. Whenever I receive a negative comment or bad review for one of my books, I distract myself by focusing my attention on something else as quickly as possible. Often, I work on the next item on my list of goals. As a result, the negative emotion soon fades and loses its ability to leave a footprint in my mind.

Since we can't think of two things at the same time or experience two emotions simultaneously, focusing on something else can be a fantastic way of dealing with negative emotions.

Identifying Your Thought Patterns

We all operate with certain assumptions about life (beliefs) and these assumptions determine how we react to what happens to us. We often go through the same patterns for years. We date the same people with the same problems over and over again or we're always struggling with money, making it and losing it. While these events may seem random and out of our control, they are often the result of our inner beliefs.

Fortunately, you don't have to run in circles like a hamster on a wheel for the rest of your life. When it comes to changing these belief patterns, the first step is to become aware of them.

An efficient way to do that is to look at your emotions on a weekly basis. Getting into the habit of journaling will help you do that. Ask yourself the following: how did I feel this week? Did I feel positive and happy or was I depressed? You can even rate yourself on a scale of 1 to 10, with 1 being your worst and 10 being your ideal emotional state.

Now, how would you need to feel to be at a 10? If you rate yourself 5 or 6 this week, why is that? What negative emotions did you experience this week? How could you work on them? Start writing down how you feel on a daily or weekly basis and you'll start to uncover specific patterns. Maybe you regularly experience specific fears around particular topics. Or perhaps you get easily depressed by criticism.

In my case, I was always worrying about the future and wondering whether I was going to 'make it.' I found it useful to focus on living in the present by doing more meditation and gratitude exercises. I also concentrated on enjoying the process, i.e., what I do every day vs. worrying about an unpredictable future.

Whenever you identify negative emotions that you experience on a regular basis, look at the thoughts and beliefs that generate these emotions. Then use the 7-step process we mentioned in Chapter 1 to overcome these limiting beliefs.

Emotions Come from Your Interpretation of the World

Have you realized that nothing has the power to upset you? The reason you experience negative emotions in any situation is that you add your interpretation to it. You may understand that intellectually, but you may not fully grasp all the implications.

When I say nothing has the power to upset you, I mean *nothing*. Reality in itself is never upsetting. It just is. The world is just how it is. You may think that the world should be different, but if it had to be different, it would be different. The only fact is that the world is as it is right now, which means that it is as it should be, whether you like it or not.

Do you remember Alice Herz Sommer, who declared that she was happy while in a concentration camp? She was content because she had a fundamentally different vision of the world and a radically different way of interpreting terrible events.

Let's do an exercise together. For each situation ask yourself how you would react and why. Finally, ask yourself, 'What would I need to believe for me to react that way?'

- Situation 1: You have a beautiful picnic planned in your favorite park on Sunday. As you're happily heading toward the park, it suddenly starts raining cats and dogs. How do you react?
- Situation 2: You're on vacation when a street artist insults you out of the blue. How do you react?

Now, are these situations upsetting in themselves? The chances are that you're pissed off and blame the rain because it's ruining your picnic. However, is the rain bothersome in itself? Is it the rain that's upsetting, or is it that you upset yourself over a completely natural event?

Ask yourself: what would I need to believe for me to react that way?

Is being insulted by someone upsetting in itself? Imagine that you were insulted in Spanish but didn't know the language.

How would you have reacted? It would still have been the same situation.

Again, what would you need to believe to react that way?

The second situation happened to me when I visited Barcelona in my early 20s. A Spanish street artist asked me if I was French before insulting me in French (hint: it had something to do with my mother). It was so unexpected that I couldn't react. I went blank and stayed in a state of shock for a few hours.

It's our expectations that dictate our emotional reaction to specific situations. The situation in itself is never the problem. It can never be upsetting by itself, even in the worst-case scenario. You must add your particular judgment for a situation to become upsetting. There must be thoughts crossing your mind that will trigger emotions. Now, could you choose to think differently? Absolutely.

In 1963, Thích Quang Đú'c, a Vietnamese Buddhist monk, burned himself to death. He was protesting the persecution of Buddhists by the South Vietnamese government. Journalist David Halberstam recalls, 'As he burned he never moved a muscle, never uttered a sound, his outward composure in sharp contrast to the wailing people around him.' I don't know how he did it, but he couldn't have had the same thoughts or interpretation of the event that we would have. He must have trained himself so well that he could distance himself from the pain associated with such a tragic event.

Of course, this doesn't mean that you're going to wake up tomorrow unaffected by everything that happens to you.

However, it does mean that you have more control than you think regarding what happens to you. The bottom-line is this: many of your emotional reactions come from your assumptions about how things should be. The way you interpret events, and how you feel about them, will change if you alter your assumptions.

Understanding How Emotions Serve You

As we've seen previously, negative emotions are the result of our interpretations of events. By choosing to interpret an event differently, we can change our emotional reaction. However, this does not mean that negative emotions are wrong. There's no need to beat ourselves up for experiencing them; that would make things worse.

Negative emotions shouldn't be avoided, ignored or even 'overcome'. In fact, they're beneficial for several reasons:

- **Your emotions help you identify core beliefs you hold.** As previously mentioned, a feeling is an interpretation of thought. And your thoughts are often the result of a core belief that you have.
- **Your emotions signal opportunities for growth.** Each time you're afraid of doing something, it's frequently a sign that you should do it. Fear is often an invitation to get out of your comfort zone and discover your real potential. When you do something despite feeling scared, you'll typically experience a sense of relief and pride. There's nothing more exhilarating than facing your fears and doing something that you genuinely thought was impossible. It shakes your current belief system and opens up a new world of possibilities.
- **Your emotions help you let go of your ego.** Each time you get triggered and feel the need to defend yourself, the chances are that your ego is standing in your way. Ask

yourself these questions: why am I getting so defensive? What am I trying to protect here?

Your emotions are an invitation to look at the core beliefs you hold about yourself and the world. It gives you a chance to examine and question them. As such, they're one the most powerful tools you have for personal growth. Make sure you observe them carefully and learn as much as you can from them.

Practicing Mindfulness/meditation

Practicing mindfulness and meditation will help you become more aware of your emotions and progressively detach yourself from them. I encourage you to adopt a meditation practice even if you believe that meditation isn't your 'thing.' Meditation has so many benefits that it would take an entire book to cover them all. Since I can't do that here, let's take a look at some of the most significant benefits here.

Meditation:

- Reduces stress and anxiety.
- Increases grey matter concentration in the brain.
- Increases your mental strength, resilience and emotional intelligence.
- Heightens your pain tolerance.
- Improves learning and memory.
- Improves self-awareness.
- Reduces the risk of heart diseases and stroke.

Don't you feel like meditating now? Why not start with 5 minutes per day?

Your Daily Mantras:

Repeat the following mantras on a daily basis

- I have absolute control over my emotions.
- I'm beyond my feelings and all negative emotions
- They quickly disappear as I dissociate from them.

To learn in more depth how to master your emotions, refer to my book *Master Your Emotions: A Practical Guide to Overcome Negativity and Better Manage Your Feelings*.

Action Step:

Spend a few minutes completing the corresponding exercise in the workbook (XIII. Mastering your Emotions)

14

CULTIVATING JOY

'The purpose of life is to be happy.'

—Dalai Lama

Are you experiencing joy on a daily basis, or are you continually frustrated, tired, disappointed and unhappy? I believe that if we can't appreciate what we already have, having more won't make us happy.

Wouldn't you love to have more joy in your life? It isn't something that happens to us when we're lucky; it's something that we must learn to cultivate on a daily basis.

We already have so many things to be grateful for in life, but our brain is wired to take them for granted. Have you ever been excited about a new purchase you just made? Now, how long did the excitement last before you got used to your new toy? It isn't long before you take it for granted and revert to your original level of happiness.

Let's do a simple exercise: close your eyes and take a few seconds to think of all the things that you want in your life.

Now, what if I told you that you'd quickly take these things for granted once you get them and will focus on finding new things to acquire? That's what many people do: they spend their entire life chasing things, looking to get a bigger house, a better car or a higher salary, yet they never feel satisfied.

There's nothing wrong with chasing things. However, you have to realize that the things you go after won't fulfil you nearly as much as you think. So, it's better to spend time appreciating all the little things you already have in your life: the security of a home, an abundance of food, your health, your friends and family, the beauty of nature that surrounds you, etc. There are so many things to be grateful for, and I'm sure you have at least a few of these things in your life.

Practicing Gratitude

Gratitude, like everything else, can be cultivated. If you want to increase the amount of joy and appreciation that you experience on a daily basis, it's essential to implement a daily habit of gratitude.

There was a point in my life when I was unhappy. That's when I realized that it was my job to train my mind to help me experience more joy and gratitude. I did it by focusing on feeling more grateful for the things I already had. You can do that, too!

Below are a few things you can do to experience more profound feelings of gratitude.

Keeping a Gratitude Journal

Writing down what you're grateful for is a great way to train your mind to focus on the positive. Can you name three things you're thankful for right now? I bet you can. In fact, you could think of thousands.

Personally, I have a journal in which I write down positive

things that people have said about me. It may be a nice email, a great review for my book or something positive that a friend told me. I continuously update it with new things, and I like to review it every morning. It's a fantastic way to train my mind to focus on the positive.

The simple practice of writing down what you're grateful for every morning will help you experience more gratitude over time.

What about you? What are you going to write down in your gratitude journal?

Practising Gratitude Meditation

Gratitude meditation is also a great way to start your day. You can find plenty of guided meditations on YouTube, but here are a few of my favorites:

- Louise Hay's Morning Meditation
- Guided Meditation on Gratitude with Deepak Chopra
- Morning Gratitude Positive Affirmations
- Morning Gratitude Affirmations - Listen for 21 Days!

Listening to Uplifting Music

One thing I also like to do is listen to uplifting songs in the morning. They can help you generate more positive emotions and allow you to access deep states of gratitude. I especially like this song in particular: Karen Drucker's song.

Finding what works and what doesn't

We all know we should be grateful for what we have. However, knowing it doesn't help, does it? That's because being thankful is an emotion to be experienced. It's not something we can intellectualize. We have to experience it.

Feeling grateful is not easy, especially in the beginning. Repeating, 'I'm grateful for X, Y, and Z' again and again doesn't mean you genuinely feel it. The key is to keep practicing and find exercises that work for you.

Maybe you like to listen to music while doing gratitude exercises. Or perhaps you prefer guided meditations. I encourage to experiment. Pick one exercise for three to four weeks, stick to it, and see how it makes you feel.

Finally, don't underestimate the power of gratitude. Imagine if you could be ecstatically happy just for being alive. We all probably should be, but we aren't. Practicing gratitude on a daily basis will allow you to feel more grateful for what you have—even if it isn't that much—and experience a decreased need for external things.

The key here is to access your emotions and not just your mind.

Blessing

Blessing things is another great way to experience more gratitude and joy in your life. You can bless virtually anything in your life. You can bless your food every time you eat and you can bless your possessions. Interestingly enough, you can also bless seemingly adverse situations. I learned the concept of blessing things that seem unfortunate in Honore's book *Prosperity for Writers*. I found it so intriguing that I've started implementing it in my life.

There's also a quote that I love from Les Brown that says, 'Don't say "I'm having a bad day." Say "I'm having a character-building day."'

When you have a 'character-building' day, remind yourself to bless it. Our most significant breakthroughs often come after our biggest failures. You can't learn much from your successes, but you can learn a lot from your failures. The key is to accept it when we fail and consciously decide to learn from it. So what can you bless in your life right now?

Giving More

Tony Robbins says that 'the secret to living is giving' and I agree with that statement. Nowadays, we're continually trying to get more: more attention, more fame, more money, more things or more friends. Unfortunately, this rarely leads to more happiness. If anything, it leaves us unhappy and unfulfilled.

Have you ever felt good about yourself for giving money to charity or to a cause that's dear to your heart? I believe that we're naturally wired to give. Without giving to one another, human beings would have probably died out a long time ago. The more we give to others, the better we feel about ourselves.

In fact, there's an experiment in which they gave participants money that they could spend either on themselves or others. The study showed that those who chose to spend money on others experienced more happiness than those who spent the money on themselves.

In his classic book *How to Stop Worrying and Start Living*, Dale Carnegie argued that if a depressed person were to spend each day focusing on what they could do for others, their depression would cease within two weeks. While this may not be true, I can say for sure that giving to others is one of the most effective ways to increase our levels of happiness.

So, how can you give more in your day-to-day life?

Tithing

Do you give away part of your income every month?

Many people recommend that we give 10 per cent of our salary to charity, including Jim Rohn, one of my favorite personal development experts. Tithing on a regular basis helps us express our gratitude and overcome the scarcity mindset that many of us have.

Many people wish rich people would be less greedy. Well, are you unwilling to give 10 per cent of your income, or even a smaller percentage, to charities or causes you want to support right now? If so, you probably won't want to give away part of your fortune when you get rich. After all, giving to charity has more to do with our mindset than with the amount of money we have in our bank account. Many rich and poor people are greedy. Money just magnifies people's vices and virtues.

The Bible says 'Give, and you shall receive,' which could be accurate. What we can say is that the more you give away money, the more open you become to receiving it. The more you do for others, the more open you are to their reciprocation.

It goes both ways. The more you do something for yourself, the more you can encourage others to do the same. Let's say you're trying to sell a product that costs a few hundred dollars and you're prospecting new clients. If you've never invested a few hundred dollars in a product yourself, it'll be difficult to convince potential customers to buy your product. However, when you regularly purchase and benefit from products with a similar cost, it suddenly becomes less challenging. You start believing that your product isn't that expensive, and it will show in your body language, facial expression, vocal tone and emotional state.

This goes to show that being at peace with money, or anything else you want to attract in your life, will allow you to attract more of it.

The bottom-line is that experiencing more joy and gratitude in your life is an inside job. You have to decide that you're going to be happier. It starts by conditioning your mind every single day. That's why I like to start my day with meditation, stretching, listening to uplifting songs and then reading old entries from my gratitude journal. Now, I wake up happier in the morning. That's an automatic response based on the conditioning of my mind. You can do the same.

Your Daily Mantra

Repeat the following mantra on a daily basis:

- Happiness is my natural state, and I'm grateful for everything I have in my life.

Action Step:

Spend a few minutes completing the corresponding exercise in the workbook (XIV. Cultivating Joy)

CONCLUSION

I'd like to thank you for buying this book. You've made it this far, which means a lot to me. You are part of a minority of people who are genuinely committed to improving their lives. I'd like to congratulate you on your effort.

My sincere hope is that this book inspired you to make positive changes in your life and to raise your standards. I hope it opened you up to new possibilities and gave you the desire to go the extra mile, test your limits and transcend them.

I understand that this book is demanding and I don't expect you to assimilate everything in it in one read. Mastering each area of your life takes time. In fact, anything worthwhile takes time!

I invite you to go back and reread all or part of this book whenever you feel the need. We all need reminders to ensure we stay on track with our efforts and keep improving ourselves. Otherwise, we'll likely fall back into our old ways. Old habits die hard!

To be honest, this book was written as much for me as it was for you. I'll reread it myself and do my best to apply what's in it until I master it. These things are easier to write about than they are to live by. If you catch me slacking off, gently call me out, I'll be sure to do the same with you.

Indeed, changing is often hard, but it can also be extremely gratifying. The greatest joy is when we do something that we thought was impossible, thus expanding our comfort zone. As

I once read somewhere, a comfort zone is a beautiful place, but nothing ever grows there. That's so true!

You've read this far so I know you're someone who demands a lot from yourself. I also know how easy it is to blame ourselves for falling short of our expectations. I do that myself. But let's face it, nobody is perfect. You and I will fail multiple times, and that's okay. I would rather fail while pursuing what I believe in than to play it safe. Wouldn't you? Fortunately, the human spirit is one of the strongest things in the world. No matter how many times human beings fail, they can always get back up. You and I are no exception.

At times, we'll feel disappointed, frustrated, tired or even betrayed, but that's also part of the process. No one has ever achieved great things without going through hardships. The good news is that we always have a choice. We can always be bigger than our problems. I started this book with a quote from Jim Rohn, so I'd like to finish with another of his quotes: 'It's not what happens that determines the major part of your future. What happens, happens to us all. It is what you do about what happens that counts.'

I wish you all the best with your future endeavors. As for me, I'll keep pursuing my journey and producing more content that (hopefully) will serve and impact you in some way.

I'm looking forward to connecting with you in the future, so feel free to email me at any time at thibaut.meurisse@gmail.com.

Also, if this book helped you in any way, please share it with your friends and family, and don't hesitate to let me know how things are going for you. I'm always happy to hear from my readers. It makes me feel less lonely and motivates me to produce even better work!

Connect with me on Facebook at:
https://www.facebook.com/whatispersonaldevelopment.org/
Talk to you soon,
Thibaut Meurisse

Do You Want More?

Learn to overcome negativity and experience more positive emotions in your life with my book *Master Your Emotions*.
Check out the preview on the next page.

MASTER YOUR EMOTIONS—PREVIEW

'The mind in its own place, and in itself can make a heaven of Hell, a hell of Heaven.'

—John Milton, poet.

We all experience a wild range of emotions throughout our lives. I had to admit, while writing this book, I experienced highs and lows myself. At first, I was filled with excitement and thrilled at the idea of providing people with a guide to help them understand their emotions. I imagined how readers' lives would improve as they learned to control their emotions. My motivation was high and I couldn't help but imagine how great the book would be.

Or so I thought.

After the initial excitement, the time came to sit down to write the actual book, and that's when the excitement wore off pretty quickly. Ideas that looked great in my mind suddenly felt dull. My writing seemed boring, and I felt as though I had nothing substantive or valuable to contribute.

Sitting at my desk and writing became more challenging each day. I started losing confidence. Who was I to write a book about emotions if I couldn't even master my own emotions? How ironic! I considered giving up. There are already plenty of books on the topic, so why add one more?

At the same time, I realized this book was a perfect opportunity to work on my own emotional issues. And who doesn't suffer from negative emotions from time to time? We all have highs and lows, don't we? The key is what we do with our lows. Are we using our emotions to grow? Are we learning something from them? Or are we beating ourselves up over them?

So, let's talk about your emotions now. Let me start by asking you this:

How do you feel right now?

Knowing how you feel is the first step toward taking control of your emotions. You may have spent so much time internalizing you've lost touch with your emotions. Perhaps you answered as follows: 'I feel this book could be useful,' or 'I really feel I could learn something from this book.'

However, none of these answers reflect how you feel. You don't 'feel like this,' or 'feel like that,' you simply 'feel.' You don't 'feel like' this book could be useful, you 'think' this book could be useful, and that generates an emotion which makes you 'feel' excited about reading it. Feelings manifest as physical sensations in your body, not as an idea in your mind. Perhaps, the reason the word 'feel' is so often overused or misused is because we don't want to talk about our emotions.

So, how do you feel now?

Why is it important to talk about emotions?

How you feel determines the quality of your life. Your emotions can make your life miserable or truly magical. That's why they are among the most important things to focus on. Your emotions color all your experiences. When you feel good, everything seems, feels or tastes better. You also think better thoughts. Your energy levels are higher and possibilities seem limitless. Conversely, when you feel depressed, everything seems dull. You have little energy and you become unmotivated. You feel stuck in a place (mentally and physically) you don't want to be and the future looks gloomy.

Your emotions can also act as a powerful guide. They can tell you something is wrong and allow you to make changes in your life. As such, they may be among the most powerful personal growth tools you have.

Sadly, neither your teachers nor your parents taught you how emotions work or how to control them. I find it ironic that just about anything comes with a how-to manual, while your mind doesn't. You've never received an instruction manual to teach you how your mind works and how to use it to better manage your emotions, have you? I haven't. In fact, until now, I doubt one even existed.

What You'll Learn in this Book

This book is the how-to manual your parents should have given you at birth. It's the instruction manual you should have received at school. In it, I'll share everything you need to know about emotions so you can overcome your fears and limitations and become the type of person you really want to be.

You'll learn what emotions are, how they are formed, and how you can use them for your personal growth. You'll also learn how to deal with negative emotions and condition your mind to create more positive emotions.

It is my sincere hope and expectation that, by the end of this book, you will have a clear understanding of what emotions are and will have all the tools you need to start taking control of them.

More specifically, this book will help you:

- Understand what emotions are and how they impact your life
- Identify negative emotions that control your life and learn to overcome them
- Change your story to take better control over your life and create a more compelling future, and
- Reprogram your mind to experience more positive emotions.

Here is a more detailed summary of what you'll learn in this book:

In **Part I**, we'll discuss what emotions are. You'll learn why you are wired to focus on negativity and what you can do to counter this effect. You'll also discover how your beliefs impinge upon your emotions. Finally, you'll learn how negative emotions work and why they are so tricky.

In **Part II**, we'll go over the things that directly impact your emotions. You'll understand the roles your body, your thoughts, your words, or your sleep, play in your life and how you can use them to change your emotions.

In **Part III**, you'll learn how emotions are formed. You'll also learn how to condition your mind to experience more positive emotions.

And finally, in **Part IV**, we'll discuss how to use your emotions as a tool for personal growth. You'll learn why you experience emotions such as fear or depression and how they work. You'll then discover how to use them to grow.

APPENDIX

Some common personality tests are:

- DiSC Personality test.
- Introvert/extrovert tests.
- MBTI test.
- VARK test.
- The Big Five Personality Test. The big five personality traits are openness to experience, conscientiousness, extraversion, agreeableness, and neuroticism.

Additional Resources:

DiSC Personality test
https://www.tonyrobbins.com/disc/
DiSC Official Website
https://www.discprofile.com/what-is-disc/overview/
Introvert / extrovert
http://whatispersonaldevelopment.org/what-doest-it-mean-to-be-an-introvert-everything-you-should-now-about-introverts
MBTI Official Website: https://www.mbtionline.com
The Big Five Personality Traits:
https://en.wikipedia.org/wiki/Big_Five_personality_traits
VARK
http://vark-learn.com

List of Healthy Products

Below is a list including some of the healthiest products on earth (in no particular order). It's not an exhaustive list, but a list of healthy products recommended by many experts. Remember that there are no bad vegetables and that most fruits are healthy. The list is based upon the following resources:

- The 150 Healthiest Foods on Earth, by Johny Bowden, Ph.D.
- Harvard Medical School
- Mayo Clinic
- Medicalnewstoday.com
- Healthline.com
- Bembu.com

Vegetables

- Broccoli
- Spinach
- Sweet potatoes
- Asparagus
- Bell peppers
- Carrots
- Cauliflower
- Cucumber
- Garlic
- Kale
- Onions
- Tomatoes
- Avocados

Fruits

- Apples
- Bananas
- Blueberries
- Oranges
- Strawberries
- Lemons
- Kiwis

Fish and Seafood

- Salmon (wild salmon, not farmed salmon)
- Sardines
- Shrimp
- Trout
- Tuna

Meat

- Lean beef
- Chicken breast
- Lamb

Beans

- Green beans
- Kidney Beans
- Lentils

Nuts

- Almonds
- Chia seeds
- Coconuts
- Macadamia nuts
- Walnuts
- Peanuts

Grains

- Brown rice
- Oats
- Quinoa

Oils

- Coconut Oil
- Extra virgin olive oil
- Flaxseed Oil (just don't cook with it.)
- Macadamia nut oil

Drinks

- Green tea (and tea in general)
- Fresh vegetable (and fruit) juice
- Pomegranate juice
- Water

Herbs and spices

- Cinnamon
- Garlic
- Ginger
- Oregano
- Turmeric
- Vinegar

Others

- Dark chocolate
- Yogurt
- Eggs

AFFIRMATIONS

In this section we're going to discuss how you can use affirmations effectively.

- **State your affirmation in the present tense and avoid the word 'not'.** Say 'I'm wealthy' rather than 'I'm not poor'.
- **Use your body and vocal tone when speaking.** This will add power to your affirmations.
- **Use visualization.** This will allow you to experience what accomplishing your goals would be like. It will also enable you to generate feelings that are in sync with your affirmations.
- **Use words or sentences that you would use in the real life.** This will make the affirmation feel more real.
- **Imagine talking to your friends.** Choose affirmations that would fit seamlessly into a conversation.

For example, consider saying the following things to a friend:

- Example 1: Yes, I'm an excellent writer. To be honest, I'm one of the best writers I know. I'm inspiring so many people to make positive changes.
- Example 2: I'm the type of person who's always taking action. I get more done in a day than many people do in a week. I've been so productive it amazes me.

Now you might not say these things word-for-word, you might think it sounds as if you're full of yourself. Even so, these can be used as affirmations and could, in fact, be part of a normal conversation.

Now, let me share some phrases you can use to help eradicate some of your limiting beliefs.

I used to be.... but now **I allow myself** to....

Example: I **used to be** shy, but now I **allow myself** to be more and more confident with each passing day. I'm reaching new levels of confidence that I've never experienced before and it makes me feel great about myself.

Other Books by the Author

Crush Your Limits: Break Free from Limitations and Achieve Your True Potential

Goal Setting: The Ultimate Guide to Achieving Life-Changing Goals (Free Workbook Included)

Habits That Stick: The Ultimate Guide to Building Habits That Stick Once and For All

Master Your Emotions: A Practical Guide to Overcome

Negativity and Better Manage Your Feelings

Productivity Beast: An Unconventional Guide to Getting Things Done

Success is Inevitable: 17 Laws to Unlock Your Potential, Skyrocket Your Confidence and Get What You Want from Life

The Greatness Manifesto: Overcome Your Fear and Go After What You Really Want

The One Goal: Master the Art of Goal Setting, Win Your Inner Battles, and Achieve Exceptional Results

The Passion Manifesto: Escape the Rat Race, Uncover Your Passion and Design a Career and Life You Love

The Thriving Introvert: Embrace the Gift of Introversion and Live the Life You Were Meant to Live

Wake Up Call: How to Take Control of Your Morning and Transform Your Life